Frank

Nymphing Secrets

Frank Sawyer's Nymphing Secrets

A Series of Articles and Notes by Frank Sawyer
On How to Catch Fish Using the Sawyer Nymphs

Arranged by Nick Sawyer

With Additional Text by Nick Sawyer

Illustrations by Thommy Gustavsson

SAWYER NYMPHS LTD

Copyright © Sawyer Nymphs Ltd 2006
Published by Sawyer Nymphs Ltd
Highbank, 45 Moberly Rd, Salisbury, Wilts, SP1 3BZ
Tel 01722 334932 Email: info@sawyernymphs.com
website: www.sawyernymphs.com

The right of Frank Sawyer and Nick Sawyer to be
identified as the authors of the work has been asserted herein
in accordance with the Copyright, Designs and
Patents Act 1988.

British Library Cataloguing in Publication Data
A catalogue record for this book is available
from the British Library

ISBN 0-9550825-4-4
(978-0-9550825-4-2)

Typeset by Amolibros, Milverton, Somerset
This book production has been managed by Amolibros
Printed and bound by Lightning Source Ltd

CONTENTS

PREFACE

Frank Sawyer's Nymphing Secrets is an attempt to collate in one place the countless fishing tips and techniques that Frank recorded in his many books, magazine articles and personal notes. My grandfather was a prolific writer on all things riparian, including the fishing itself, but this caused him to bury some fundamental points and secrets among texts on much wider subjects. I hope I have managed to find them all!

When broken down to fundamentals, the Sawyer techniques equate to three basic methods:

The Sawyer Nymphs in running water.
The Sawyer Nymphs in still water.
The Sawyer Bow Tie Buzzer technique.

There are, of course, many variations to each of these themes but the fundamentals remain constant. Master these and you can truly say you are a nymph fisherman. There is something in this book for the beginner and the expert alike. I don't think anyone ever stops learning about nymph fishing and Frank was no exception. He continued to refine and adapt the Sawyer Nymph techniques until he died. He wrote articles on his thoughts and findings late into his life. The two editions of *Nymphs and the Trout* are his most well-known works on nymphs but he wrote hundreds of articles on the subject after these books were published. The best are reprinted for you here.

This book is different from the previous works of Frank that my father and I have republished. For a start it is a simple paperback, designed to be read time and time again and even taken to the riverbank as a reference piece. Secondly, we have moved away from the philosophy and theory of nymph fishing to its practical application. And finally, we have added illustrations from one of the finest contemporary fishing artists in the world – Sweden's Thommy Gustavsson.

Thommy is the editor of Scandinavian fishing magazine *Flugfiske i Norden*. I first met Thommy in 2005 when he invited me to fish the River *Storan* in Sweden. This was the same river system that Frank fished in 1959 with Nils Farnstrom – see *Nymphs and the Trout* (second edition). Not only is Thommy the most skilful fly fisherman I have ever met, he also has a magical talent with water colours and a pencil. This book doesn't really do Thommy's art justice, but nevertheless I think you will agree his illustrations complement Frank Sawyer's writing perfectly.

Good luck with the techniques and tips presented in *Frank Sawyer's Nymphing Secrets*.

Nick Sawyer
Salisbury 2006

CLARIFYING THE DIFFERENT

FLY METHODS

Based on articles from *Trout and Salmon* Magazine
– May, 1968 and *Shooting Times & Country*
Magazine January 6-12, 1977

To me it seems that the true definition of wet fly is fast being lost and there is also a lot of confusion as to what constitutes nymph fishing – so much in fact that it is difficult to write about either method without going to a lot of explanation. Today on many public waters, a wet fly or nymph can be anything and any size as long as it is cast with a fly rod, or, to be more precise, in the manner adopted for fly casting. There is no ruling either as to how the line should be fished. If you wish to let it sink to the bottom or strip it in at the speed of a motor boat, all well and good, providing this is done by hand-lining and not by the cranking of the reel handle. But where after all, is it leading us?

We have had enough confusion in the past in trying to

define wet fly. This in itself is a misleading term but at least it has its origin in flies. In many cases the old patterns which were used, and indeed still are, were but sparsely dressed versions of the dry flies which themselves were copies of the natural insects. You may wish to argue this point and say the wet-fly style of fishing was practised before the dry fly and therefore the dry fly was but a copy of the wet fly. But I cannot think this is true for I feel positive the fishermen of years ago must have used artificials to float on the surface long before they used them below it. What indeed led them into the use of wet flies otherwise?

These people were painstaking in their observations and surely must have known there is no such thing as a fly under water of the same shape as those to be seen on or above it. Yet their dressings of artificials included substantial wings and all the natural colours of the actual fly they aimed to copy. As we know, and they must have known, the colour of duns and spinners is somewhat different to that of the nymphs. Alders, sedges and so on, were all tied to look like the hatched fly and not like the nymph or pupa. This alone should be enough to clear up any doubt, if doubt does indeed exist.

The value of the wet fly, or team of wet flies, was in the way these were fished. The main attraction to fish was the dancing of the bob fly or dropper at or actually on, the surface. Many of the smaller wet flies were so sparsely dressed that when being towed through the water, the dressing collapsed to drape the hook and give the streamlined effect of a nymph. And so in fact the true wet-fly style had a combination of dry fly and nymph. The bobbing or dipping flies at the surface might well delude fish into thinking they were hatched creatures, while those which draped and dragged deeper were mistaken for nymphs. The flashers and the fancy wet flies came at a much later date. No one knew then, or even now, what they represented, or why they were taken. They were given such names as Invicta, Butcher, Zulu and so on. But still they were kept at a reasonable size and corresponded roughly with the general size of insect life and other small creatures which were to be found near the surface of the water. These might well be representations of creatures such as shrimps, corixa, small beetles and, maybe, little fish. They attracted and deceived trout and, what is more, they could be fished in the old wet-fly style.

Later still came the nymphs. There were evolved to represent the smaller types of the true underwater insects in size, colour, and shape. In most cases a single artificial served to attract and deceive the trout when they were feeding at or near the surface. Mostly these were fished with a well-greased line and with the nymph not more than a foot beneath the surface. Fish took these either as they sank after being cast, or as the artificial was being moved slowly through the water.

Being constructed in a nymph-like manner, these artificials needed very little movement and the lightest of tackle could handle them perfectly. It is true that nymph fishing calls for more concentration by the angler, for few fish hook themselves when taking the slowly moving artificial. The nymph is not a wet fly and, indeed, it calls for an entirely separate technique to the wet-fly style of fishing. A nymph can be defined as being an undeveloped insect of the kind which moves freely through the water, either when swimming here and there for feeding purposes, or when travelling to the surface to change to a fly. The largest which can come into this category is the nymph of the Mayfly. A pattern to represent this need not be more than an inch in length.

In which category, then, can we place the big lures and terrors, which are not being used in the pretext of being nymphs of flies, and which, in fact, need a completely different casting technique? Such fishing cannot be termed wet fly, neither can it be called nymph fishing. These methods, plus dry fly fishing and dapping, which is a form of dry fly, are named after the creatures the artificials supposedly represent. Let us search around for clues that may help name the fourth form of fly fishing.

There are nymphs much larger than those of mayflies – for example, those of the dragon flies, the damsel flies, and the stone flies. But do fish ever get much chance to see them as they swim in mid-water, or hatch at the surface? I think not. They are not adapted for swimming and at the time of hatching to a fly, the emergence is made by crawling up banks, rocks, or the stems of the various water plants. A nymphal representation dragged along near to the bottom might deceive a fish, and perhaps a hatching pattern at the surface could be attractive. But that is all.

What I have mentioned so far covers anything which can be related to actual nymphs, wet flies, or dry flies. But many other creatures form the food of trout, including big beetles, minnows, sticklebacks, leeches, loaches, bullheads, and crayfish. Then there are the fly of perch, roach, rudd and dace, trout fry, small eels, and lampreys. All are taken freely by feeding fish and a representation of any can be deadly if fished in accordance with the habit of the natural.

There are many representations to choose from, some of a size corresponding with that of the 'naturals', which might be three to four inches, or even longer. It is just as easy to make one of wood, plastic or metal, and often enough the general effect and appearance of the former is much better. But, just because such materials are used, this creation is called a fly, or perhaps a nymph.

How is it possible to make a distinction and to name the fourth method of fishing when such creations are used, so that in future there need be no confusion? To me it seems the word fly will have to remain, for it has been with us too long to be altered now, indeed what else can one call it? And in a way it does help to make a distinction between fly and spinning. One cannot use the word lure, as in a sense, all types of artificials are lures. And so I make the suggestion that any fishing carried out with artificials on hooks larger than size 6 should be called 'deep fly'. This would be in keeping descriptively and at the same time fall in line with wet fly, dry fly and nymph. Deep fly could then be a representation of any one of the creatures I have mentioned and others too. It would be a technique entirely separate and one which could command the kind of tackle most suited for it.

With deep fly in mind, tackle makers could then cater specially for this class of fishing and with rods, reels, lines, leaders and artificials. Writers, when describing the various fishing tactics employed, could have one more descriptive phrase to use. Such definition could also simplify rules for fishing. The size of hook could be the deciding factor. All artificials on sizes larger than size 6 could come into category of deep flies.

The deep-fly method of fishing is not one I like myself when fishing for brown trout or rainbows. But I use the technique often enough for salmon or sea trout. The so-called flies one used for these fish have no natural insect counterparts and so the term fly fishing is again a misnomer. Wet fly and deep fly in the case of salmon and sea-trout fishing is covered adequately by the terms greased line and sunk line. For these types of fishing one uses tackle constructed accordingly. The greased-line outfit cannot cast the big flies one uses with the sunk line. Neither can the ordinary nymph, dry fly or wet fly rod deal successfully with the creations used in deep fly.

When I first started to write about nymph-fishing, soon after the Second World War, I had no idea that the time might arrive when nymphs would become so popular and likely to supersede the conventional wet-flies as a means of taking fish in most of our waters about the country. Nor do I think G. E. M. Skues had this in mind, for no longer can nymph-fishing be described as "Minor Tactics". But it now appears that many fishermen have come to the conclusion that tyings which are made to conform very closely to the natural nymphs on which fish feed have a much greater chance to deceive than those which must rely almost entirely on movement transmitted by stream or rod to make the dressings drape about the hook and so transform them into something quite different from that accomplished by the fly-tyer.

This is what happens with the great majority of patterns that are tied in so-called wet-fly style. The actual dressing has little or no resemblance to any creature which can swim, or even hang suspended in midwater, and it is not until movement is imparted that the artificial takes on a shape with some conformity to a creature which can move freely beneath the surface and so appear natural to a fish.

There is no such thing as a fly – that is, a fly with wings and legs – which can swim beneath water in a horizontal plane. Though it is true there are a number of different kinds which can submerge for the purpose of egg laying, none of these can go beneath water unless it has something on which it can crawl downwards. For the most part these flies cling very tightly to whatever substance on which they have chosen to make the descent, and, should any mischance occur, when the hold is broken and they become free, they are buoyed very quickly to the surface by air in the body and by some trapped beneath their folded wings. In static water such an ascent is almost vertical, but in a running stream a certain drift might occur before the surface is reached. Even then these insects need some substance to which to cling and crawl before they can break through the water film and so return to the air. Only then will the wings unfold again. The point I wish to make about these is that no attempt is made to swim. Perhaps, while these egg layers are beneath water, they could be described as wet-flies, but not I think in the sense which was meant when the first artificials were constructed.

I know a lot of fishermen maintain that some of the wet-fly patterns are made so that the wings, and the hackles representing the legs, can open and close as the artificial drags through the water. Some advocate a sink and draw, or lift and pause, method of retrieve, to allow this to happen and so that the fly can show life as the wings and leg-fibres move. But I have never seen this happen with any of the wet-fly patterns I have constructed, or with any I have used which have been made by others. My experience is that the soft materials one normally uses in the construction merely become bedraggled as soon as the patterns become soaked, and, when movement through the water is imparted, the water pressure causes all the dressing to stick to the hook or to whatever body material has been used.

If you cast a wet-fly, or team of wet-flies, into static water and just let them hang stationary, few fish are likely to be attracted to them and even less to take. Fish do not expect to see dead and bedraggled flies floating about in mid-water and become suspicious when they do. But it is very different when a drag movement causes the dressing to close up and take on a nymphal form. The dead and bedraggled creature is quickly forgotten. When casting downstream or across a current in a river, it is far more simple, because then a drag commences and a closing up of the dressing occurs as soon as the line and leader straightens to cause a pressure.

Anyhow, I think I have written more than enough to explain the point I wished to make when I started this article

– which simply is to question the need to make artificials with wings and legs and which to us look like flies, when what the fish expect to see are tyings which conform very closely to the form of nymphs. Why not construct nymphal patterns in the first place and then fish them in an imitation of nymph behaviour? Though it is true that many fish have been caught with wet-flies, and no doubt many others will be taken in the future, it is not because the actual art of the fly-tyer has deceived them.

Patterns which, to fish, look like nymphs the moment they enter the water are far more likely to attract and deceive than any which have to be transformed, and so a decided advantage is to be gained. Fish will take a well made nymph pattern even as it sinks or if it should hang stationary in mid-water. No fast movement through the water is desirable and there is no need for sink and draw, or for lift and pause. Just a slow and even drag will give all the movement that is required.

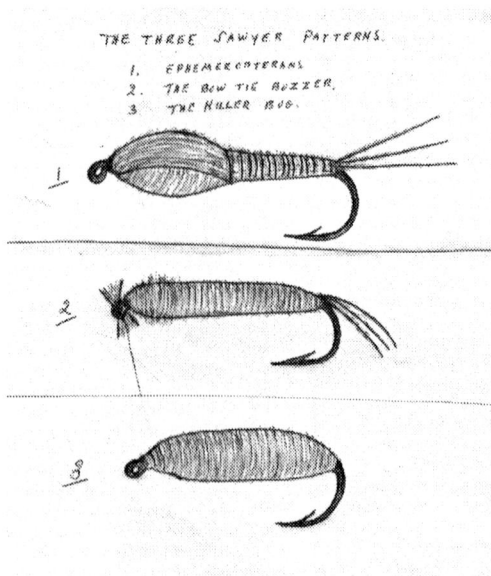

An original drawing by Frank Sawyer of his nymph patterns.

Years ago I came to the conclusion that no fibres are necessary to suggest legs on artificial nymphs for, as I explained in my book *Nymphs and the Trout*, when nymphs swim, their legs are held in streamline form, and therefore should not be noticed by fish, or if so, only as part of the body. Time has proved this to be true for today the "Sawyer" patterns are used throughout the world and many thousands of fish have been deceived by them.

Nymphs tied in true nymphal form are much easier to construct than any patterns of wet-flies, and though perhaps the finished articles are not so spectacular to look at from the human point of view, it is the fish that must act as the judges.

Swimming and hatching nymphs.

THE WAY OF A TROUT WITH A NYMPH

Based on a series of articles from
Shooting Times – 1975

Though it is now well over 20 years since my first book *Keeper of the Stream* was published, to be followed in 1958 by the initial version of *Nymphs and the Trout*, and in 1970 by the second, I still receive a lot of questions even from those who have read all three books. So it would seem that, despite my efforts to write simply and with clarity, what I have tried to convey with the written word has not yet been fully understood. Before my own books dealing with nymphs and nymph fishing were published there were several more, the classic examples being the work of Mr G. E. M. Skues. There have been others since. Yet it would appear that there is still some uncertainty about just how a fish reacts to an artificial nymph and the exact moment to tighten in order to get the hook home.

I believe there are a lot of fishermen who still think that

fishing a nymph is similar to fishing a team of wet flies or stripping in big lures. Yet nothing is further from the truth and, if you really are to have success with true nymphing tactics, then the sooner the other kinds of fishing are forgotten, the quicker a bag will be filled. Nymph fishing must be considered as an entirely separate art, and methods, to be proficient at it, must be adapted accordingly. This means that you must dismiss from your mind most of what has been learned with the dry fly, wet fly and lure-stripping practices, and concentrate on something which is quite different. As I have said, and indeed written many times, once the penny drops, so to speak, nymph fishing becomes the most artistic way by which fish can be caught, or so I think.

Most people who can cast a line to deliver dry flies, wet flies, etc, can also cast a nymph in a way that is likely to attract some feeding fish, at least. But in the great majority of cases with those who are learning, it is after the nymph is presented that failure occurs. Failure comes in some cases by not knowing just how to use a rod to make the offering look lively and attractive, and secondly, which is by far the most important, in knowing that the fish has taken the offering. So many, who have fished in other ways, think they must see some disturbance at the surface, as is the case when fishing floating flies, or to feel a decided pull on the rod tip which leaves no doubt that a fish has taken, as happens when fish take offerings such as wet flies and lures fish with a decided drag beneath the surface.

My object in writing now is to recap on some of the more important explanations I tried to offer in my books, and, in fact, to stress the few things which I consider to be the fundamentals of successful nymphing. Foremost of all these I would say is good eyesight and quick reflexes, for so much must depend on noticing just what happens, and acting immediately. Concentration and anticipation must come second, for even if you have good eyesight and reflex action, neither is of any use unless you are intent on your fishing and expecting a take. In this respect one might say that nymphing can be more tiring than any other style of fishing. The reason is that there is so little to see, and only by watching very intently can any indications register.

Casting and the general presentation of a nymph might be called mechanical, and the delivery of an artificial in an accurate and delicate manner must depend on one's ability to use a rod. One thing, however, must be kept well in mind. Casting is just a means of getting the nymph to the feeding position of a fish. It is true that this is important, but it is what happens just after the cast has been made that counts. It is at this point, and in the subsequent few moments which follow, that a lot of fishermen fail, and many a fish is missed.

You should bear in mind the fact that, from the moment a well-made artificial touches the water and sinks, it has attraction and therefore might be taken immediately by a fish in that locality. So the angler must be watching and ready for action. Much, though depends on the class of fish one is after and the general habitat, so for nymphing there can never be any hard-and-fast rules. Anglers have to adapt themselves according to circumstances. For instance, the technique one adopts when fishing chalk streams and other clear waters where fish are easy to see, might be deemed easy in comparison with places where fish are invisible to the fisherman. Yet in both the nymph has a somewhat similar attraction for the quarry. In one, however, you can actually see the reaction of a fish and the take of the artificial; in the other imagination has to play a big part.

Though it is extremely fascinating to be able to see a trout, cast accurately to it, and watch as it takes, all this is very evident. You are able to judge the exact spot to pitch in the nymph and all the while have the quarry in view. You can see the moment the fish moves to intercept and indeed the movement of his jaws as he is deceived into taking. It is then up to you to tighten at the precise moment that the jaws are closed. If you miss hooking him, you know it is your own fault, or that of a faulty hook. This is because you have seen what has happened.

But fishing blindly as I call it – that is, to fish which are not visible – can be a somewhat different story and, as I have already said, this is where imagination must play a part. But it is difficult to imagine anything that has not actually been seen. People who can do this are few and far between. You might say that inventors have this gift, but it is seldom that inventions turn out in the way they were first conceived. Maybe it was because most of the nymph fishing I did years ago was in clear water, where I could see all that took place, which gave me a great advantage when the time came to try for those which were invisible to me in the rivers, lakes and reservoirs. The repeated deception and the watching of all that took place both beneath and above the surface, as I fished for both trout and grayling, became firmly imprinted in my mind.

One of the things I learned very quickly when I started nymph fishing, and after watching the efforts of other fishermen, was that to interest a fish it was necessary to get the artificial down to the level of its feeding position, to where, in fact, the fish expected to see such prey. To do this called for a lot of experimental work, both in the construction of various imitations and in the manner of presenting them. It was not until I had the idea of using fine copper wire as ballast and for tying in the dressing that this obstacle was successfully surmounted. Then I found that, to have nymphs which would sink and fish correctly at different levels, a variation in weight was necessary.

For a while I persevered with different ballast with the same size hook, this being just a light covering for fishing near the surface and becoming heavier as depth increased. But I found that the extra weight for deep water fishing ruined the general shape and symmetry of the artificial, and that it no longer conformed to the delicate requirements I needed. Then I hit on the idea of tying the same pattern on different sized hooks, small for fishing near to the surface, medium for mid-water and large for real depth. For some reason which I cannot explain, the deeper one fishes, the larger can be the artificial. Whether fish can see better near the surface than close to the bottom will always be a mystery, but what I did prove was that a pattern quite double the size of its natural counterpart was effective at depths of three feet or more, though it was useless to offer it near the surface. However, this solved the problem for me. I would carry patterns on the varying sized hooks and fish these as the occasions demanded.

To get a nymph to penetrate and sink through the water quickly called for a change in my general style of casting. Hitherto, most of my fishing had been with the dry fly, when the object was to place line, leader and fly on to the surface as delicately as possible so that the fly would ride well cocked and leader and line would float well. Though I found that it was just as important for line and leader to be on the surface, I had to work out a way in which the nymph could enter without making too much disturbance. This was just a matter of checking the smooth flow of the shooting line as it extended horizontally over the water; it had the effect of making the nymph curl downwards, when it would enter the water before the leader and line fell. I have described this very thoroughly in my books, but I mention it now because such presentation can help considerably in all classes of water. Today, far more anglers fish still-waters than streams, and I have found that since I started nymph fishing in lakes and reservoirs the practice has served me well.

Some people think they stand a much better chance of catching fish if they use more than one nymph on a cast. With this I cannot agree. Though I tried it on various occasions just to satisfy myself on this point, I came to the conclusion that there is far more lost than gained. It is as much as I can do to cast a single nymph properly and then use my rod to make it look lifelike. And I would think this must apply to all fishermen.

In most river fisheries where dry fly and nymph fishing is permitted, the rules are that one fly, or one nymph, must be used, and this usually in an upstream manner. But in many of the still-water fisheries, small and large, the angler is allowed up to three, sometimes more, on a cast. In some cases there is no ruling laid down as to what size of hook may be used, or what length of lure. One is also permitted to use varying types of lines – some designed to float, some for mid-water and others to go very deep to work the flies and lures along the bottom. Through the years many fish have been caught with these recognised methods of wet fly and lure fishing, and in the future many more will be taken. For those who are happy to catch fish in this way, all well and good.

But I cannot refrain from saying that I think a lot of good sport is wasted, for I have proved many and many a time that, with few exceptions, when fish are really on the feed, they are far more likely to take a small offering than a large one and, if they are alert and looking for food, a single artificial fished well is far better than several fished badly. When heavy lines and a team of artificials on a leader are used, one can hardly say there is any delicacy in the presentation, indeed it is impossible to use outfits of this kind in the same way as when offering a single. Again, though it is possible to use a rod to make one nymph fish in a lifelike way, two or more cannot be given the same animation.

The success of an artificial nymph underwater depends on several factors. First, it has to be reasonable copy of a kind of nymph which is seen and taken readily in the natural state. Second, it must be delivered in such a way that it sinks quickly and does not scare the quarry, and third, and this I think is of the greatest importance, one must be able to transmit movement to it by the use of a rod.

For a start, let us examine what is meant by a reasonable copy of nymph seen and taken readily. With trout, as indeed with all creatures, including the human, certain foods have more appeal to the palate than others, and these appear very regularly on the menu, so to speak. This is what one might call the staple diet, and traces of it can be found whenever an autopsy is carried out. For trout, certain classes of nymphs are for more acceptable than others; for one reason, one might assume that their food value is high, and for another, that these types are frequently to be seen where they can easily be intercepted and taken.

When you start to talk or write about nymphs in our waterways you enter a very fascinating yet complex subject. Many fishermen think that the term nymph can cover any artificial dressed in nymphal fashion and fished underwater. Yet this is far from true. For some reason which I have yet to understand, the word "nymph" only applies to certain aquatic insects and only to these during the last period of their existence beneath water when, in fact, the wings have become fully developed in their cases and the time for emergence as a winged creature approaches. So there can be confusion.

Why indeed should all the mature under-water insects

of the *ephemeridae* species be called nymphs, yet those of the *diptera,* for instance, be termed larvae? Further examples can be the *odonata* and *perlidae,* (dragonflies and stoneflies) being described as nymphs and yet *trichoptera* (sedge flies) as larvae. All transpose from underwater to winged form in much the same way, in so much that each is fully developed in the aquatic state and each casts an integument, or slough when changing to a fly. As I have said, all this can lead to confusion and it needs far more explanation than I can give here.

In all my talks and writings on nymph fishing I have tried to be explicit about the use of the word nymph, keeping it in its proper context as the great G. E. M. Skues and others have done in the past. Here I repeat what I have written elsewhere: "To get the utmost enjoyment for the technique I employ it is necessary to use artificials which can be cast delicately and accurately with a light rod and line. Indeed delicacy in the whole outfit is the aim to be pursued and achieved, or much of the joy, and indeed the fascination of nymphing is lost."

I feel very doubtful if nymph fishing would ever have been registered as a sporting method of taking chalkstream trout and Skues advocated the use of the larger types which can be found in the majority of our waters. Nymphing in lakes and reservoirs had not been practised then – perhaps not even thought about – and there was little data to hand which dealt with the general fauna in them.

Skues must have known, as most of us know, that the trout in the chalkstreams and other rivers feed on many different kinds of underwater creatures, both large and small, and he knew the habits of the majority. Perhaps he made copies of many of the nymphs, etc. which he found in autopsies, and trying them, just as I did, but after much trial and error concluding that it was only the swimming group

17

of nymphs which could provide the answer to his requirements.

Today things have changed a lot, and maybe we are not quite so fussy as fishermen were in the days of Halford. Even so I feel sure that Skues was right when he chose to disregard the large sized nymphs and concentrated on those which could be made so that they looked delicate and attractive, and at the same time be easy to present to a feeding fish.

Swimming nymphs, as the name suggests, are creatures which can move freely through the water in much the same way as fish. Included among them are several different genera, each of which has a number of species which vary in size and in colouration. Among the better known to fishermen are those of the olives and iron blues, spurwings and pale wateries.

To make copies of all the species in this swimming group one would need at least 20 different tyings, each on the appropriate hook size, but after years of trial and error I came to the conclusion that such a number was quite unnecessary. Indeed I found that I had wasted a lot of time, a lot of patience and a lot of materials and in the end gained very little. Also I found that having so many different artificials tended to be confusing. It was then that I started a process of elimination and reasoning.

In the end I reduced the number of my patterns until but two were left. One to represent the dark types, the other the lighter ones. These I named after the materials used in the construction. Neither is an exact copy of any known nymph, merely a blending of materials – simple materials – which could incorporate a little of each of the species and bring about a general effect, when fished in the correct manner. These I called Pheasant Tail and Grey Goose, the former to represent the olives, iron blues, etc, the other for the pale wateries. Each can be made in the various sizes required.

Though there is importance in having the right colouration and size it is the general effect seen by a fish that counts. As I have written in a previous article, one of the essentials is to construct a nymph pattern so that it can penetrate the surface and sink to the level of a feeding fish. It was because of this, and because I knew fish would not expect to see the legs of a swimming nymph, that I decided that no hackles or other materials were necessary to suggest legs. This served two purposes: one to make construction more simple, the second so that there could be no obstruction to quick sinking.

The main features which were obvious to me when watching mature nymphs, were the swelled wing cases and the use of the tail for propulsion, coupled with the general stream-lined effect. On these I based the tying and appearance

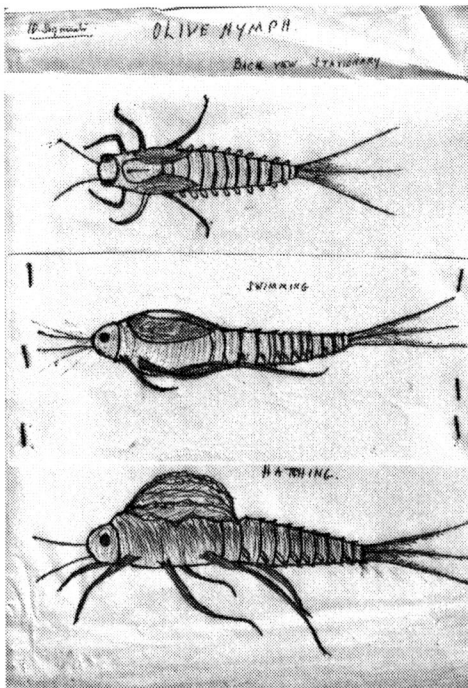

Some of Frank Sawyer's early nymph drawings.

of my patterns, on the assumption that what I could see must also be seen by a feeding fish.

Nothing can really look alive unless it moves, and trout expect to see movement of one kind or another in most of the natural food they take. If you care to study the currents of a running stream you will see many thousands of varying particles drifting with the water, both in and on it. Even as you see them, so these are seen by trout. To you, many of these particles – bits of weed, leaves, sticks and so on – might look very much like a nymph, or some other sub-aqueous creature, but the fish ignore them. From a very early age, indeed from the time trout fry start to feed, it is the activity which denotes life that they look for. And if you wish to deceive them, this must be kept well in mind.

An artificial nymph, if ballasted correctly, can attract as it sinks. Trout expect this to happen with naturals and the falling movement is sufficient to arouse interest. But much greater interest will come when a sinking artificial starts to swim to one side or another, or moves upwards towards the surface. This natural movement can be imparted with a rod and in later articles I will be dealing with it.

Time is never wasted when one studies fish on the feed, and through the years I have spend many hours doing this. Such studies can be both extremely interesting and educational, proving beyond doubt that fish have an intelligence far greater than many fishermen realise. Though trout have well-developed senses of smell and indeed touch, these are very secondary to sight. Without keen eyes, fish would slowly starve. The instinct to note movement and react accordingly is a natural one bred in them, and it is something which cannot be eliminated by artificial methods of rearing. In this respect the stew-bred trout, providing they have lost none of their natural eyesight while in captivity, are as quick to react as those which are wild.

When trout position themselves in a running stream it is with the main intention of feeding: to intercept and take food carried to them by the water current. And so, when one is seen poised at any point between the bottom and the surface the odds are greatly in favour of this being a fish which can be interested with imitations of the food he is accustomed to seeing and taking in such a position.

Trout can be placed in three classes. There are those which take up stations close to the bottom, those which position themselves in mid-water and those which can be seen close to the surface. The first are fish which are interested mostly in what happens on, and near to, the bed, the second which feed on mid-water classes of food, and the third are those whose main interest concerns what is happening in, or on, the surface. Though all will take a correctly presented artificial, it is the mid-water class which is most likely to become victim of the nymph fisherman. These are what one might describe as the real nymph takers – interested in anything around, above or below.

In his writings, Skues dealt mostly with fish which positioned themselves near to the surface. He had studied those which were feeding on nymphs nearing the process of eclosion – hatching nymphs, in fact – and his patterns were made to be fished in, and just beneath, the surface. The absence of any real ballasting incorporated in the dressings confirms this. To get his nymphs to sink to a depth of a foot or more, where they might attract the mid-water feeding fish, meant that they had first to be thoroughly wetted or anointed with glycerine, spit, mud, or some other agent. Actually Skue's method of nymphing was very much on a par with upstream wet-fly fishing, a technique which had been practised for a very long time in many waters about the country.

One might say, therefore, that the real art of nymphing

has developed considerably during the past half-century and the "Minor Tactics" have become the "Major Tactics" in many of the erstwhile dry-fly waters. I can't think that Skues ever dreamt this might happen, and to be quite honest, neither did I, when starting to write about nymphing myself. The band of nymph fishermen has increased to the stage when I feel very doubtful if there are many who go fishing nowadays without a supply of nymph patterns in their boxes. All have learned that fish can be caught and that, providing the right tactics are employed, sport with the nymph can equal, and indeed surpass, any that can be had with a dry-fry.

Correct tactics have to be employed if there is to be success. First the approach, then the presentation of the nymph, high, middle or deep, so that it can look lifelike to a fish. Following on from this is spotting the take, and finally hooking, playing and landing the quarry.

As I have said and written many times, a cautious approach and placing of a nymph is of the utmost importance. A fish, frightened by the sight of you and your rod action, or by the fall of line, leader and nymph will never take confidently and, in the case of a really wild fish, is often scared badly and bolts for cover. Even if one should stay in position, all repeated attempts at deception are to no avail. The first cast is the one that counts, that first placing of the artificial and the artistry in making the dead appear alive.

Often a well constructed nymph will attract as it sinks and drifts and, providing it is presented so that if falls close to the stationed fish, the fish will take without suspicion. The falling from suspension coupled with something which, in shape and colour, looks like a nymph, gives the fish good reason for thinking it is indeed an edible creature, like others it has taken in similar circumstances. Unless a stream or river is in flood, or carrying a very strong flow of water, no heavy particles are carried in suspension, and there is no fallout. Fish know this and, when seeing something falling towards the bottom, think it is well worth investigating if it bears any resemblance to food.

This kind of presentation can bring results, but a much greater attraction is when the nymph is made to check in its descent and start to move to one side or the other, or upwards, as though swimming. Then any suspicion, any doubts which are in the mind of the fish are quickly dispelled. Here, he thinks, is something that really is alive and in a flash there is the urge to take.

The art of the nymph fisherman is to be able to create this illusion, and it is well within his power to do it. But it needs perfect judgment and timing. Judgment in casting so that the nymph can sink to the level desired and then the timing of the imparted movement so that this can take place just as the offering comes within easy taking and eyesight range of the quarry.

The rod movement to impart animation should neither be fast nor jerky, but merely a gathering of all slack with the line control hand, followed by a slow even lift of the rod tip with just sufficient speed to make the nymph swim. When trout can be seen in the water it is quite easy to judge the correct depth and nymph movement. And then it is fascinating to watch the reaction of the fish one is trying to deceive. If you are watching closely it is possible to tell the very moment the artificial is sighted and to be prepared for what follows.

Though lots of factors go into the build-up of nymph presentation which are of equal importance, the greatest part of all is in knowing when a fish has taken, and to be able to hook it. Even though there is faultless delivery and animation of an artificial to achieve deception this, and anything done well previously, is of no avail unless one can tighten at the correct moment so that the hook can take a hold inside the jaws of the fish.

When one is fishing a nymph correctly, only an occasional fish will hook itself. Hooking must be done by the fisherman in much the same way as when using a dry-fly. The only difference is that the nymph is taken beneath the surface where there is far less to indicate this. A fish taking a dry-fly riding high on the surface cannot possibly do this without poking his jaws through to the air and at the same time causing a rise form, or ring, as it is sometimes called. The dry-fly man who is intent on his art will see the artificial taken in the jaws and is wise to pause sufficiently to allow the fish to turn down before lifting his rod to tighten the line and set the hook. There can never be any hard and fast rule to follow; speed in hooking must depend on the speed a fish takes to turn down. In this respect, fish rising in fast water are much quicker than those in slow parts; and again small fish are far more active than large ones. Much the same thing can be said about the take of a nymph. Takes can be fast; they can also be slow and very deliberate.

Tightening, striking, or just plain hooking, as one might well call it, is a matter of reflex action, a co-ordination, or synchronisation, of eyes, brain and hands – a combination of practice and training until the whole thing becomes automatic. In the past I have compared hooking with rifle and shotgun shooting. Just as there is that moment to release the firing pin and send the shot or bullet speeding on its way to connect with the target, so the tip of a rod must be moved to tighten line and leader, and move the hook sharply enough to make the point penetrate and hold.

Success depends on when, and how, this is done. A great deal must centre on the kind of tackle one is using. A slow actioned rod and heavy line cannot possibly react as quickly

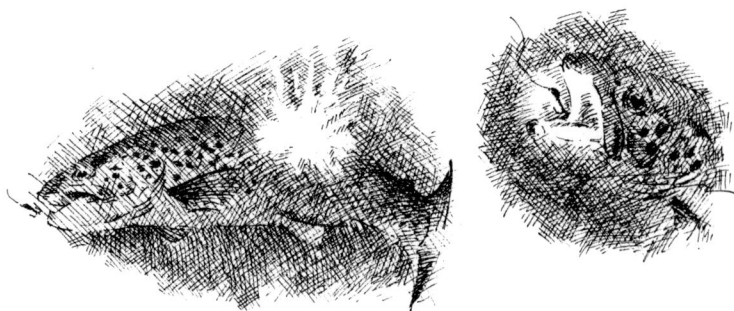

Visual take signals – watch for a flash of underbelly of the white of a mouth opening.

as a fast actioned type with a light line. A long rod will pick up line much faster than a short one. And so it is a case of adapting one's action accordingly, and there can be no general rule to be observed.

It is because I have seen many hundreds of fish take a nymph and then be missed by the fishermen that I make no apology for repeating what I have said and written many times. You just cannot allow your attention to wander – even for a moment. Only those who are really concentrating will see most of what does happen, for even the best of nymph fishermen will fail to observe everything.

Even after many years of nymph fishing I still miss chances to hook some fish for they are so quick in taking and ejecting I have to confess to being beaten. But, taking a general average with trout, I can say that I definitely hook, or touch, at least four out of five. Some come unstuck afterwards it is true, just as they do in all forms of fishing. This, one must accept and attribute to bad luck, caused, in fact, by the hook hitching into soft tissue and tearing free under stress.

What you must watch for in nymphing is the check, or draw, of the floating leader, and for this it is essential to have a line which floats well and a leader greased for at least half its length. Without this visual aid one is lost. You could have a hundred takes with a submerged leader and line and not realise that a fish had been anywhere near to your nymph. I repeat that in nymphing a take by a fish is rarely registered on the rod. To put it more plainly, you don't feel your fish. The take, like that in coarse fishing, is registered by the movement of the float, the float in this case being the leader just where it enters and sinks beneath the water.

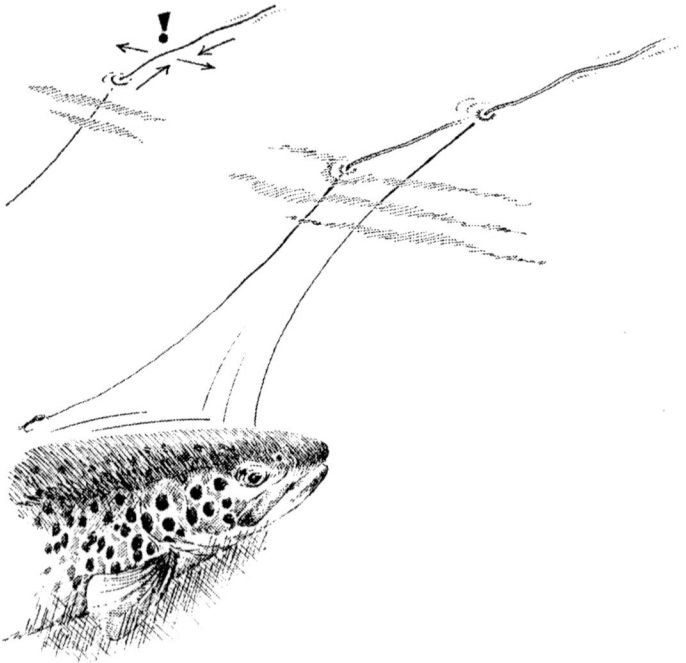

Watch for a slight check or drawing under of the leader.

Through the years I have explained and demonstrated this to a large number of fishermen. Often, by not striking, I let pupils see just how quickly a fish can eject an artificial nymph. Though I have likened the float business to coarse fishing, there is a lot of difference. Coarse fishermen have the advantage of using natural baits, or edible baits, as one might call them, and fish taking these will hold them in their mouths much longer than anything that is artificial.

To give just one instance of what can happen I recount a few hours spent with one would-be nymph fisherman, on a series of small lakes. Other than to say that these lakes were stocked frequently with big rainbows, they shall be nameless. It was very obvious to me that a large number of fish had recently been introduced, maybe very early that same morning.

These big rainbows were cruising about in small shoals, taking anything which looked like food, or which showed some sign of life, and there was a slight ripple on the water. I greased line and leader and put on a Killer Bug. I would like to explain that my pupil had fished these lakes on five different days in the past month and failed to catch a fish, while many of the other fishermen had taken their limit of five. The reason was soon obvious. He had done quite a lot of dry-fly and wet-fly fishing and could throw a very fair line.

His first cast was a good one and the line and leader had barely settled on the water before I saw the draw down of the point, but my "Yes!" brought no response from my pupil. He had seen nothing. Two casts later another fish took. Again the failure to act. "Show me," he said. I took the rod, told him to watch intently, and made a cast. As I gathered up the slack and lifted the rod tip, so the greased leader slid beneath the surface. A flick of the rod and the fish was on. But it was another wasted effort – he maintained that he had seen nothing. It was two hours later, and after I had counted 20 missed fish, that he finally saw what had been so plain to me. During this time I had caught another in a futile attempt to show him just what happens, and this left him but three for his limit. Maybe it was an extra hungry fish which took them, for the cast drew down in no uncertain way and he saw it and acted in a perfect manner. "Got it," he said. "Now I know." And he did, for without any further coaching or help from me, he took his last brace without missing a take.

DECEIVING A NYMPHING TROUT

Based on an article from the *The Field Annual* 1951

On South Country chalk streams, I think that by the use of the nymph in the daytime during the months of July and August you can reach the peak of the fascinating sport of trout fishing. At this time it calls for the highest skill of both the wet and dry-fly fisherman, and to them the nymph fisher brings every wile at his command into the true art of deception.

I often read in old books of the great bags of trout taken by such anglers as the Rev. Durnford and Colonel Hawker when fishing the chalk streams with wet flies, but I feel sure that both these great fishermen, and many others of their time, would have enjoyed far more sport in catching less fish had they known of the art of trout fishing as practised today.

In the spirit of Francis Francis:

> *No murderous wand*
> *Would I command,*

That slaughters but for slaughtering's sake
But win by skill
Enough to fill
The wants that Nature's self doth make.

To my mind, the great joy in trout fishing comes with the knowledge that you have deceived a trout into taking an imitation of the natural insect on which it happens to be feeding. If the fisherman is a fly-tier there is added pleasure, for in the occupation of making an artificial, he will be filled with the anticipation of seeing his creation accepted by a trout in mistake for the insect he has been at such pains to copy. In imagination he will be by the riverside, see the trout moving without suspicion towards the hook his nimble fingers have so artfully concealed, see the mouth of his fish open and close, and in advance get the thrill as, in his mind, he lifts the rod to drive home the hook.

An artificial nymph can be used with deadly effect throughout the trout season, but I think it is only during the months of July and August that it can give the fisherman the highest degree of sport, and the knowledge that he is accomplishing something beyond the powers of the ordinary wet or dry-fly enthusiast. During these two months the water of our chalk streams is usually at its clearest. There are days of sun blazing from cloudless skies, when not a breath of air disturbs the surface of the river; when it is possible for the angler to see every movement of a trout in the water, and, conversely, for the trout to see every movement of the angler, unless he uses the greatest caution in approach. Truly these are the days when the utmost enjoyment of nymph fishing can be obtained, for trout already have had a severe hammering with the dry-fly and most of them have a good knowledge of the fisherman and wiles.

At this time the wild trout of a river are really wild; the

brilliant sunshine and unruffled, gin-clear water, gives them the opportunity to see every artifice the fisherman may present. Though a few flies hatch daily from the river, the clear dry atmosphere allows them to change quickly from nymph to dun; they leave the water almost immediately, and seldom give trout the chance to rise and take them from the surface. Yet trout are lying up in the water and are feeding; and a feeding trout can be caught if he is offered a good representation of the food he is taking. It is quite obvious that he is not feeding on surface borne food, so it must be on something under water.

A very long experience has left me astonished at the failure of fishermen to take the trouble to learn what flies may be expected on the water throughout the fishing months. Some do not even know that duns change into spinners, and cannot tell the difference between one and the other, even when held in the hand. I have encountered anglers who do not know that most of the river flies spend most of their life under water and that fish take them in various stages of their existence.

I think the late Mr. G. E. M. Skues, whom I met once or twice towards the end of his life, got the greatest joy in fishing, from the practice of deception, at which, indeed, he was a master. He spent years studying the various insects and in learning from others all he could about them. He tied flies beautifully, and he had an immense collection of them. They were made with the most careful attention to detail, of size, colour and general appearance, and he had great success with them. He was a man who understood something of the trout's angle of view. He paid great attention to the body of the fly, and his pattern was not encumbered by overmuch hackle. When fishing he would take a fly off the water – a fly he had reason to think the fish were taking – study it thoroughly, and then search through his fly boxes for the most exact imitation. I believe that in fifty years he had hardly ever thrown a fly over a fish, which he had not tied himself. In this, I am sure, consisted a large part of his enjoyment.

Mr. Skues understood the art of nymph fishing, and in his excellent book *Nymph Fishing for Chalk Stream Trout,* he tried to pass on his knowledge of this fascinating sport to others. He knew where to look for a fish and, what is more, he knew what the trout expected to see. And here is the true art of deception. It is in knowing that a fish is expecting to see a certain insect in a certain area, and in being able to place an artificial at this point without raising suspicion; it is in having a clear view of a feeding fish so that you can study its reactions to what you offer it. Times without number I have been amused to see a trout discover the deceit, to watch the fish move boldly towards my artificial, then sheer away at the last moment and bolt for cover. I then know I must make something better and I get joy in doing so.

The great thing is to offer the fish something he is expecting to see. If he is rising and taking surface flies, then he should be tempted with a dry-fly; if he is nymphing, then he should be offered a nymph. But with the dry-fly you have an advantage, for it is possible to see the natural insects floating on the water and to get some idea as to which kind the trout are taking. It is not difficult to tell the difference between such flies, as, say, the Blue Winged Olive and the Lesser Spurwing, and to be able to determine a black midge from an Olive. Yet a trout may be taking one or other of these beneath the surface in their larval or nymphal form and there is little to tell he is doing so.

This is where a slight knowledge of entomology can be of assistance to the angler, for if he is familiar with the habits and appearance of these insects underwater he then stands a much better chance not only of presenting the right fly at the right time, but of presenting it in a manner that is life-like. Though a good copy of an insect is essential, this is not always enough, one should know what the trout expect this insect to do, and be able to show it to them in this light.

I once made some copies of the B.W.O., and, when comparing them under the microscope with the natural insect in water and looking at the body, had difficulty in telling the two apart. I was exceedingly pleased with my efforts and, as Blue Winged Olives were then hatching, I tried them on the trout. I had tied them so that they had a good entry into the water and, on being presented, they immediately sank towards the bottom. Though two fish made a move towards one of the nymphs, six or seven more totally disregarded them. I failed to get a fish to take any I had made. I could not quite understand it, for I had often deceived trout with Iron Blue and Olive patterns fished in a similar manner.

Then it occurred to me that the Blue Winged Olive swims to the surface in a jerky, undulating movement; that, once it has risen to hatch, it seldom returns to the bottom but often stays wriggling in the surface film for a few moments before hatching to a fly. Good as my artificials had seemed to me they had not deceived the trout. These fish knew there was something wrong in my presentation. I then also knew what it was and went home to make other patterns. The trout wanted something which showed life near the surface of the water. They should have it.

I used exactly the same materials for a body as I had for the previous patterns, but instead of adding a few turns of fine copper wire to the hook to make it heavy, I dressed my new copies as though I were making a dry-fly. My rejected patterns had been finished with a soft hen hackle at the head, but these new ones I dressed with a cock hackle and then cut off the fibres so that they stood out rigid from the thorax. My one idea was to make an imitation that would sink just through the surface film, and appear to the trout as though it had spread its legs and tails in an effort to hold itself up in the water. My finished efforts pleased me.

When cast lightly, like a dry-fly, the artificials did as I wanted, and sank just beneath the surface; and, in sinking, the stiff cock hackles, spread one from another with the action of the water and appeared like the moving legs and tails of the nymph I had copied. Six trout took my offerings. I could have hooked them all, but I did not want to. I had sufficient pleasure in deceiving them.

I have said I could have hooked them had I wished, for if you are to catch fish with an artificial nymph the hook must be driven home by the angler — it is very unusual for a trout to hook himself. In this respect the art of nymph fishing differs greatly from the wet-fly method, for in wet fly, the idea is to cast the artificial across, or downstream, so that the action of the water plays the fly, or flies, and in so doing, given them an appearance of life as they move through the water. To get the utmost enjoyment while nymph fishing, the representation should be cast upstream to a trout this is visible to the angler; a fish calculated to be of a reasonable size. There is no indiscriminate fishing of the water, searching the likely places and in general using a chuck and chance it method, and of tightening when a fish is felt.

Though you may not be able to follow exactly the progress of an artificial nymph in the water after it has sunk, you can have a good idea of its relative position when nearing the trout. I would say good eyesight is a most essential part of a nymph fisher's equipment, for without it he would be advised to stick to the dry-fly. I have seen hundreds of fish missed by striking too late, or too early.

Often there is not the slightest indication on rod, line or cast that a trout has taken a nymph into its mouth. The angler has to rely entirely on his own powers of perception; be able to see the fish move towards the artificial, and to see it open and close its mouth. With the dry-fly he has the advantage of seeing the fly floating on the water and, even if the artificial cannot be seen, the rise form made by the trout is sufficient to tell him the fish has risen. In most cases it is possible to see the head of the fish as it breaks the surface, and the precise moment of lifting the rod to tighten is at once apparent. In nymph fishing there are also times when the trout can be lured upwards to that it takes near the surface as, for instance, when fishing the B.W.O. nymph, but far more often the trout are taking the natural insects at depths which vary from six to eighteen inches, when they take so slowly and so gently that no disturbance to the surface is caused by their moving bodies. An artificial must be fished down to them.

There is, in the late Dr. J. C. Mottram's book, *Thoughts on Angling*, a most surprising statement, which shows, at all events, that, at the time he wrote, he had no conception of the proper way of taking trout on a nymph. This is what he says: "If I wish to give a novice or a duffer his best chance of catching a trout on a chalk stream, I remove his dry-fly, soap half his cast, and tie on a nymph." He goes on to say: "Other things apart from drag make fishing easier; the hooking of the trout is simpler and more sure, though drag alone answers our question. Nymph fishing is much easier, is, therefore, a less delicate art, and, therefore, gives less sport."

All I can say in reply to this is that I am a river keeper and, as such, I am not likely to advocate a method by which a stock of trout can be sadly depleted. A gamekeeper would not suggest that the pheasants he had reared could be killed easier on the ground or while they were at roost. He would be far more likely to arrange drives where his birds could be presented to the guns as high targets, and at a variety of angles – where, in fact, they could be killed in the most sporting manner. And so it is with me. I like rods to kill trout, but I also like them to get the utmost enjoyment in doing it.

Dr. Mottram may possibly have been thinking of wet-fly methods. It is of such importance that nymphs should be used legitimately, that I make no apology for repeating that they should be thrown only to a particular fish, a fish that is obviously taking sub-aqueous food, and not cast at random. Only if this done, can the angler get the full savour from his skilful deception.

Perhaps when the art has been thoroughly acquired it will seem easy – the same can be said of every sport – but in the learning of nymph fishing you can spend a lifetime and still find there are trout that are not deceived by your best efforts. As I have said earlier, a little knowledge of entomology can be of great help. If you know a certain type of insect is being taken by a trout, and know that it is the habit of the creature to swim from one weed bed another just beneath the surface, then a presentation can be made accordingly.

Most of our trout flies spend one or two years under water in their larval and nymphal stages and during this under-water life are taken freely by fish. But there are many different species which have habits that are greatly at variance. Some spend their under-water life in the river-bed, some live under stones and cling to them like limpets; others crawl about on the river-bed and in vegetation; and still more range freely in all places and can swim like little fish.

Some of them prefer one type of water, some another, some hatch at the beginning of the season and others at the end, with still more in the intermediary period. They are of varying sizes, shape and colouration, and when hatching into flies each species has its characteristic method of approaching the surface. For instance, the mayfly nymph, the largest of them all, swims direct from the river-bed to the surface to hatch; trout seldom see it in larval or nymphal form until it is nearing the surface to change into a fly. I am not, by the way, suggesting the use of a mayfly nymph representation – far from it. When trout take hatching mayflies they will also take floating flies, and I consider the use of an artificial mayfly nymph to be, to put it plainly, little better than poaching.

But in converse to the mayfly we can take the Olives, or the Spurwings. There are several species of each of these genera, and they have habits that are similar. Their larvae and nymphs are of the swimming group – that is, they can move from point to point, by swimming freely through the water like fish. They live on the river-bed, on vegetation, and may be found everywhere, at varying depths. But whereas the Olives prefer well aerated water, the Spurwings like water of a sluggish nature. They may make journeys to the surface long before they are ready to hatch into flies, and return once more to a lower level. They may move through the water from one feeding place to another and, in a score of ways, form an attraction the trout find hard to resist. Trout know of the habits of these insects, and of all the others, and position themselves in places where they can easily take them.

As further examples we have such flies at the Little Yellow May Dun – the Turkey Brown and the Claret Dun. These are seldom seen by fish while in their larval or nymphal stages. They spend their life clinging to substances on the river-bed, they are seldom found in mid-water, and when hatching to a fly they crawl up the banks – on vegetation, or anything which extends from the river bed to the surface.

An artificial nymph of either would, therefore, be useless fished in mid-water, and I am doubtful if there is anyone in the world who could make one appear to crawl up a weed stem.

It is very difficult to explain the varying habits of all these nymphs, and I have no space to do so here, but I would like to suggest that during the trout season an hour or two could be very profitably spent by the would-be nymph fisherman in studying the under-water habits of the insects he wishes to imitate. The actual nymphs are quite easy to obtain in any chalk stream. A fine meshed net run through a bunch of ranunculus near the surface will produce many mature nymphs of the kind most suitable to copy. They can be carried home in a small container and will, if kept moist, retain their colours perfectly for at least twenty-four hours.

If you can sit in a boat, or stand in waders near the down stream end of a weed bed, or at a point where a clear view of the river-bed can be obtained, and look closely into the water, a considerable movement of insect life will soon come into view. I have often lain for hours on a river bank near a bunch of weeds, with my nose nearly touching the water, and have had flies hatch so near to me that I could have taken them in my mouth. In this and other ways, I have discovered the identity of the various larvae and nymphs. I have seen their movements in the water as they feed and sport, and the various methods they have of approaching the surface to hatch into flies, and I have seen trout take them in all stages. Only by knowing what a trout expects to see can the true art of deceiving them be accomplished.

NYMPHING IN STILL WATER

Based on an article from *Trout and Salmon* –
November 1961

The art of nymph fishing in lakes and reservoirs is becoming more and more popular and I foresee the time approaching when the old and well-tried method of fishing a team of wet flies will be abandoned in favour of the single nymph on a cast tapered to a fine point. A light, well greased or non-sinking line, with rod and reel to suit it, will make up the outfit. Only in recent years have I come to know and really enjoy the sport there is to be had in fishing the still waters. I must confess that previously I thought that the catching of trout in lakes and reservoirs was a poor substitute for river fishing.

How wrong I was, and how mistaken are those who still hold such views. However, much of what I learned about nymph fishing in rivers for trout and grayling has helped me considerably when adopting a similar technique in the still waters. My fascination for this kind of fishing was clinched for me when I spent a fortnight in the mountain lakes of N. Sweden. There I had plenty of time at my disposal to work out theory into practice. So when I fished again in the lakes of this country I was able to go at it with quite a different approach and with success fresh in mind.

My wife cannot understand why I like to visit Chew Valley, to travel a distance of 60 miles and then pay a pound to fish when trout are plentiful in the water I look after and in other parts within easy reach. From her point of view perhaps it is rather amazing, for no doubt there are many who fish at Chew Valley and other reservoirs and lakes who would love the chances I have to fish rivers.

I would not go to any of the lakes if I had to fish a cast of wet flies or monstrous lures which need a heavy line and a powerful rod to cast them. It was only after I found by much perseverance that is it possible to get good sport with light tackle and a single nymph, or lure, that I began to class it as exciting and interesting. Trout in lakes will take small nymphs and lures quite as confidently as those in the running stream. But the whole secret of success lies in the ability of the fisherman to place the nymph where it can be seen by a fish, and in such a way that the fish is deceived into thinking it is a natural creature.

With lake fishing I have come to the conclusion that it is nothing but a waste of time to cast indiscriminately and search an area of water unless one or more fish have shown themselves at the surface. Even then there is little reward if these fish are not moving regularly. By this I mean a rise form here and there at intervals in the water which can be covered. To catch lake fish with nymphs the trout must be feeding in the upper foot or so of water, indeed not below the depth to which the nymph or lure will sink, and where it can be given the required movement.

The important thing is to know that there are fish within reach. In rivers it is possible, in most cases, to see fish and even if they are not to be seen, if one rises you know he is likely to be still in the position. What is more, in the running stream you know very well in which direction the head is pointing and therefore can deliver the nymph accordingly.

In the lakes the trout continue to move, to search in fact, and in so doing will travel about over a very large area. But their search is a thorough one and to me it seems very possible that each fish selects a certain beat and keeps to it for a while. On various occasions I have found that if I note the area of a rise form and continue to cast to that spot, the same fish can be caught there even though he has many acres of water around him.

At times it might mean casting to that one place for ten minutes, or even longer, but eventually patience is rewarded. One can only imagine what these lake fish are doing. To me it seems possible that they cruise on a long beat which might take them along the shore for a considerable distance, or perhaps the beat takes them out towards the centre of the lake. At some point they reach a territory worked by other fish and so the return is made.

The big trout at Chew valley are no longer the easy fish they were during the first two seasons this lake was opened for public fishing. At that time, as in many other stocked reservoirs, newly opened, the fish would take almost any lure or wet fly which showed some sign of life as it was dragged through the water. Many of course, had to forfeit their lives as a result but others escaped with an education which I feel sure has been communicated to other fish now living in the water. I don't think it is wise to underrate the reasoning powers of fish, or for that matter any wild creature, and though it may sound silly to say they can warn one another of danger, I feel they can advise each other as to what is good to eat.

And so today it is necessary to use artficials which very closely resemble, both in shape, colouration and movement, the kind of animals on which trout feed when they rise to the surface. As in rivers the fish have a large variety to choose from and the stomach of a trout can contain up to a score or more of different creatures. But there are some animals they like much better than others and when these are seen they are taken regardless of whether it is just an isolated appearance or not.

In a previous article I wrote some time ago in *Trout and Salmon*, I described some success of myself and a friend at Chew Valley when we caught fish with a lure I devised many years ago to take grayling in the chalk streams. Then I said I thought the lake trout took this because they thought it was a hatching sedge, the rising pupae of the brown silverhorn. Now I feel confident that I was right in assuming that. Since that time I have been to Chew Valley on different occasions throughout the season and each time I have fished with confidence, a confidence I inspired into the friends who went with me. We all caught fish, I knew we would as we were offering the trout a representation of one of the creatures they see and take frequently.

The grayling lure does indeed delude the lake trout into thinking it is a hatching sedge. But the general shape and colouration is not enough. These lures must be fished correctly or much of the attraction is lost. I found this to be true when fishing them to grayling. Occasional fish will take the lure as it sinks but the majority are attracted when a movement is imparted to the lure by the fisherman.

This movement is not a haphazard one. It should be made in a cool and calculated way when imagination must play a big part. First you must know a little of what the trout expects to see. With the hatching sedge, this is the insect coming up through the water to hatch. It is seldom that these come up vertically and often they will swim along just beneath the surface for a few yards before emergence, looking for a place to cling, such as a weed stem on which they can crawl to the air and then hatch. A study of these creatures among the weed banks around the margins of lakes can give one a good idea of their habits. Compared to the nymphs of the *ephemeroptera*, the speed of movement is sluggish. They have a slow and rather laboured effort made on an even plane – a movement which can very easily be simulated by a fisherman using his rod in the right way.

Because I honestly think the grayling lure is a good example of the hatching silverhorn sedge when presented correctly I once again give details of its construction. I use hooks in sizes, 10, 12 and 14. In each case additional weight is given to the hook by an even winding of 5 amp fuse wire or any copper wire of similar size. Over this wire a treble winding of wool of the colour shade I have mentioned before as being Chadwicks 477. This can now be obtained from Messrs. Veniard, of Thornton Heath, Surrey. The finished effort is not much to look at, indeed one might say it is crude. The colour changes when wet.

However, though the correct colour shade is very important, more important still is the manner of fishing the lure. As it moves through the water so the crudeness of construction vanishes. There is certain translucency in the wool fibres. The colour shade and movement, combined with the grub-like appearance brings life to the artificial and an eagerness to take to any trout within sight of it.

First, as I have already written, find a place where fish are showing. Use a quick-action rod with a light line and leader tapered to a point fine enough to allow quick sinking of the artificial. Grease the line well and also the butt of leader. Cast the lure to the area where a fish has shown. Continue to cast if necessary but each time watch the floating line and cast butt. Watch to the point where the leader enters and disappears beneath the water.

These instructions will possibly bore those who already know and adopt the technique. But each day others are keen to learn anything which might help them towards some spot. For these I must write with some clarity. The heavy lure sinks quickly. Pause a moment or two after casting, a period calculated to allow the artificial to sink about two feet. Then with rod pointing low over the water, gather in all slack line until a drag commences. Then slowly lift the rod tip whilst continuing to gather in line. Sometimes the take of a fish is felt and a quick flick of rod tip will set the hook, but more often the take is indicated by a draw on the floating cast butt, or line — a kind of reverse of the arrowhead which shows as the free line moves towards one as it is being gathered in. Quick action with rod tip is then essential but this is not as difficult as it might at first appear. In lifting the rod to impart a drag, the rod comes into a very easy position, in fact it is already flexing with the pull of the line so that instant contact can be made by a flick of the wrist.

In this kind of fishing it is necessary to use fine cast points. The finer the point, the quicker the lure will sink and the more attractive it will appear beneath the surface. The fine point allows more wobble or action of the artificial. With the fine cast point it is essential to have a light line and rod, a rod with a sensitive tip which will flex to the wrist action needed in hooking. Some may say that you cannot hope to land the big fish of Chew Valley with light tackle. With this I strongly disagree.

But different tactics must be adopted. The moment a big fish is hooked he should be allowed to run if he so wishes. Just hit him, hold the rod up so that it flexes to the pull and let the reel run. A hundred yards of 10 lb breaking strain nylon does not take up much room on a reel. If a fish wants to run that distance then let him. It is doubtful if he will. Usually he pulls off about 50 to 80 yards and then the drag of the long line slows him up. When he stops, a quick recovery of line can be made, and it is very unusual for a second and longer run to be made. If the hook has been driven home when the fish takes it will continue to hold. The light tackle means one has to be careful and the playing out of a fish may take a little longer before it can be brought to the net.

When fishing at Chew I use the same rod and line I use for the more delicate fishing of nymphs in the chalk streams indeed, excepting for a slightly stronger cast point the outfit is identical. With this I get great enjoyment, and at the end of a day a feeling of satisfaction that I have treated the lake fish with the same respect I show to the wild trout in our rivers.

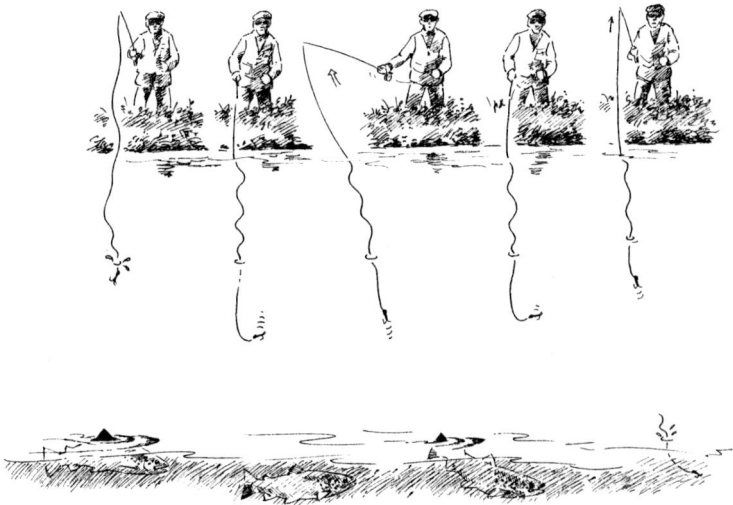

"How to nymph in still water."

THE SAWYER KILLER BUG

Based on articles by Nick Sawyer
and Frank Sawyer

As far as I am aware, no one is really sure why the Killer Bug is so effective. My grandfather originally designed it to imitate the freshwater shrimp *Gammarus Pulex*, but it is just as effective in water without the crustacean, or when tied several times larger than is natural. The Killer Bug is usually taken when it is made to 'swim'. More often than not this will be in the 'shrimp zone' but it can sometimes be taken above this area while apparently 'swimming' to the surface. As shrimp only inhabit the bottom part of a chalk-stream it is difficult to see why the fish would take an artificial shrimp in the wrong place. Pigs may fly, but who would eat a bacon sandwich if it was floating several inches above the table? Frank Sawyer suggested in *Nymphs and the Trout* that the swimming bug resembled a hatching sedge making its way to the surface. Some quite well-known fishermen claim the Killer Bug looks like a maggot or a grub that has fallen into the water, others say it looks like a food pellet to stocked fish. I have even seen small pike follow a Killer Bug through the water (although never take) so perhaps it resembles a small fish under some conditions.

The freshwater shrimp –
Gammarus Pulex

A hatching sedge

The widely reported chalk-stream malaise and decline in fly abundance is a definite cause for concern, but we sometimes forget that perhaps up to 80 per cent of a trout's food is taken sub-surface. Unless we are lucky enough to be fishing during a hatch, the trout may not be that interested in dry fly. This presents a problem. Like most fishermen, I fish when I can find the time, hatch or no hatch. Fortunately fish have to eat. If there is no surface fly, or they seem to be ignoring any fly and hatching nymph that are present, then they must be eating something else. It is often the freshwater shrimp.

It is always amazing how often fishermen fail to spot the huge number of clearly discernible fish in a stretch of water. The first step in Killer Bug fishing is to try and operate where the fish are visible. It is not essential, but it makes the technique easier and much more fun. Seeing fish is not an inherited skill, it has to be learnt. I was lucky. My childhood was spent with my grandfather and father giving

me a hard time every time they pointed to a fish I couldn't
see. I tried lying but got even more grief when I couldn't
say how big or what species the fish was. Needless to say I
soon learnt to spot them. With hindsight, and the benefits
of military training, I now realise that seeing fish is simply
a case of self discipline and patience. It is very easy to throw
a quick glance over the water without really looking. To
search water for fish, we have to remember that we are
looking through the river surface at a volume of water with
a number of layers, each with quite different optical properties.

The Upper Avon, where I enjoy most of my fishing, has
a grayling population that far exceeds that of trout. It is
very tempting to ignore the grayling and keep moving
upstream on the hunt for trout. My grandfather had a phrase
for this: "Giving up gold to fish for tinsel." Grayling are a
true wild fish and a joy to catch. Not only do they provide
worthy sport, but they taste good and are more plentiful
than trout. On many occasions I have been fishing for
grayling and a previously hidden trout has darted out of cover
to take my Killer Bug. For the out-of-practice fisherman,
or those of us who fish infrequently, grayling are an ideal
way to start the day and polish up those Killer Bug skills
before tackling the big trout a few hundred metres upstream.
My father and I sometimes make a day out of grayling fishing
with a Killer Bug. The goal is to catch every single grayling
in a shoal before moving on. It is not unusual for us to
land well over 50 grayling in 3 or 4 hours of fishing.

The most important part of the Killer Bug technique is
making the bug swim in the correct manner at the right
place. To achieve this, the bug must be allowed to sink to
the bottom part of the river and then made to swim up to
the surface in a smooth, natural manner. Where to start
the swimming motion will depend on the location of the
fish and the current flow. The point at which the swimming

motion commences is known as the activation point. The cast has to be made far enough up-stream of the activation point so the bug can sink to the right depth before the swimming motion is started. This point is known as the cast area. Here's the good bit. As long as there are no weeds or obstructions, the bug can bounce along the bottom for some distance before commencing the swimming motion. This reduces the requirement for accurate and delicate casting as anywhere upstream of the cast area will be satisfactory. All the fisherman has to do is allow the bug to bounce along the river bed until it reaches the activation point and then start the swimming motion by slowly lifting the rod tip and maintaining a tight line. The peculiarities of weed, obstructions and currents can occasionally prevent the fisherman from carrying out this technique, and fish have a habit of feeding in awkward places, but there will be many locations on the chalk-stream where this technique can be used. Trout can sometimes be startled by a bug rolling along the river bed but grayling are hardly ever troubled.

The activation point is easy to calculate. To be most effective the Bug should be made to start swimming 1 to 2 feet in front of the target fish. This makes the activation point 2 feet in front of the target fish if it is located at the bottom of the river, or further upstream if it is feeding nearer the surface. The cast area will depend completely on water depth and current speed. Unless it is a particularly deep pool or a very fast current, 4 feet is a good starting point, but trial and error will ultimately be the deciding factor. If it is clear that the bug has not sunk to the bottom before the activation point, move the cast area further upstream. (See Diagram).

Knowing when to strike is without doubt the hardest part of Killer Bug fishing. I have seen fisherman draw in their line and cast again, blissfully unaware that several fish have taken, and then spat out, the Killer Bug. The strike is easiest when the fisherman can see the bug and fish clearly, but can also be made when just the fish is visible. It is even possible to use the line at the point where it enters the water as a strike indicator and the very best Killer Bug fishermen can be successful by striking on instinct alone.

With good light conditions and clear water it is very easy to see bugs in the water and even easier to see the fish. What could be simpler than watching the Killer Bug enter the fish's mouth and then striking? Unfortunately fish spit out bugs very quickly and the act of striking can take a long time in comparison, particularly if the fish is a long way off or there is a lot of slack in the line. That is why Killer Bug fishing is more successful close in; it removes the need to anticipate the fish's action. If the fish is more than 15 – 20 feet away, the strike will have to start before the fish has taken the bug due to the time lag between striking and the hook being set. Fish very rarely hook themselves on a Killer Bug.

The Killer Bug Technique

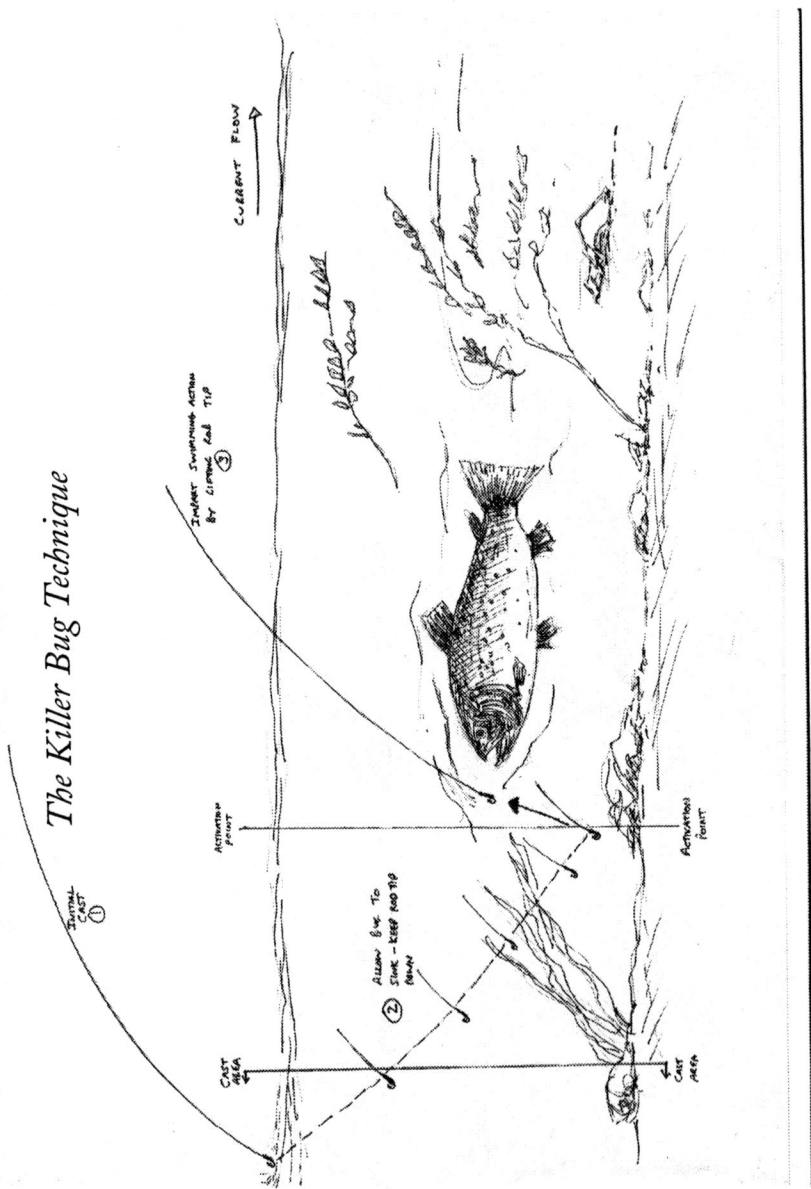

It is also relatively easy to judge when a bug has been taken by watching the fish. This is the more common technique as it is very difficult to keep watching a tiny Killer Bug as it sinks several feet away. Although you may be unable to see your bug, you should have a reasonable idea where it is located in the river. Any fish that runs towards that rough location and then stops may well have taken. This is the time to strike. If your cast has been very accurate the fish may not have to move that far to take your bug. In this case look for a flick of the tail, a sudden move of the head or a slight upward tilt. Ironically, inaccurate casting, which causes a fish to move to your bug, is sometimes more successful as it can be easier to identify the take.

Occasionally it is not possible to see either the fish or the Killer Bug. Perhaps the river is too dirty or the light is wrong. In these conditions it pays to watch the line at the point at which it enters the water. When the bug is swimming, watch for tiny, almost imperceptible checks or movement at the point where the line dips beneath the surface. If you see such an indication, strike. Occasionally the fish will take with a thump and there will be no mistaking the act, but this is rare.

Fishing on instinct alone is the most difficult of the techniques, but really it is just commonsense and experience. Commonsense dictates that the Killer Bug is most likely to be taken in the first few seconds of the swimming action while in the 'shrimp zone'. Experience tells us that grayling and trout are predictable: most fishermen know the places where they are likely to feed. Combining commonsense and experience leads to an instinct for where and, more importantly, when a fish is most likely to take. Striking at this point may result in success. It is certainly worth a try if it is not possible to use any of the other techniques.

No matter how you caught the first fish it is important

to 'slime' the bug, nylon cast and leader. Fish slime has several properties which are extremely useful to the Killer Bug fisherman. Firstly the slime makes the bug taste more natural. This causes the fish to take more time in spitting out the artificial, giving valuable extra milliseconds in which to strike. Slime on the cast 'wets' the nylon and allows it to slip through the water more easily. This makes the bug sink quickly and force is imparted along the line with less water resistance. Finally, slime masks the distinctly human smells, such as soap or tobacco, which are left in minute traces on everything we touch.

There are no promises in fly fishing but a competent Killer Bug technique on the chalk-stream is as close as one can get to a guarantee while still adhering to club rules. The technique is simple, effective, great fun and, once mastered, it is never forgotten. The Killer Bug's biggest attraction is arguably its versatility. With today's hectic lifestyle, the associated pressures on valuable fishing time, and the notable decline in fly-life and surface feeding, it is perhaps more relevant to modern fishermen than ever before. After more than 50 years of distinguished service, the Killer Bug remains a deadly enigma, and long may it remain so.

Author's Note

Although this article concentrates on the Killer Bug, any of the more modern shrimp derivatives and 'Czech' nymphs can be fished in the same way. Their effectiveness in comparison to a Killer Bug will, I'm sure, elicit some strong views and passionate arguments. It will ultimately be a question of personal choice, but beware of flies and nymphs that are tied for the fisherman's eye rather than the fish's. The success of the artificial will depend on what it looks like when wet, at the bottom of the river, to the eyes of a suspicious fish.

How to Tie a Killer Bug

Not only is the Killer Bug fishing method very simple, the tying of the Killer Bug is also easy. All that is required are hooks (size 12, 14 or 16), thin copper wire, wool (preferably Chadwick's 477, but any light grey natural wool will suffice) and a small amount of fly-tying varnish. If the bugs are tied well there is often no requirement for varnish. Don't be put off by the Killer Bug's scruffiness – this is part of what makes them so attractive to fish. The bugs have a hairy and untidy look when dry, but when wet take on a whole new colour and persona. The wet wool becomes almost translucent and the hairy wool 'wiggles' during the swimming motion. The four simple steps for tying a Sawyer Killer Bug are given below:

1. Wind the copper wire evenly around the shank of the hook starting at the hook bend. Make sure that the initial end of the wire is secure. A covering from the hook-bend to hook-eye and back again is about right. Leave the wire dangling from the hook-bend.

2. Starting at the hook-eye, lap a length of the wool along the hook covering the wire, stopping at the bend. One covering of the wire is usually all that is required, but if it is particularly fine wool a double or triple covering may be required. The ends of both the wire and wool should now be located at the bend of the hook.

3. Take the wire and bind the end of the wool in place with two or three tight turns of wire. Snip the ends of the wool and wire and, if necessary, put a small spot of varnish on the ends to set them in place.

You may remember reading of some success I had when fishing a grayling lure to trout at Chew Valley Lake ("A study In Contrasts" in the May issue of *Trout and Salmon*). What there is about the colour and construction of this very simple bug, I cannot say, but now I recount another story of fishing a larger version of it to salmon.

I made mention of this grayling lure and the taking of a 15 lb fish in my book fish in my book *Nymph and the Trout*. Since I wrote this there have been other occasions when I have found the lure to be attractive but I did not have the chance to try out the technique thoroughly until a day in the middle of June of this year. This day was the most amazing and exciting one I can remember, even though my luck was out.

Friends of mine have a beat on the lower Hampshire Avon around Ringwood. On this day the beat included the bridge pool in the town of Ringwood – a pool well-known to fishermen and indeed to the public. After early June, when the water is low and clear, it is possible to see salmon from the bridge parapet.

SEVEN FISH

We arrived at the pool about 10.30 a.m. The sun was high, the light good and no wind. My first glance showed me two fish and then after a closer scrutiny I saw five more. These varied in size from one of about 10 lb to a really big fish estimated by the keeper to be between 35 lb and 40 lb. These seven fish were well known. They have been in the pool a long time and on most days one or another of those who had beats had tried for them with all the usual methods, including prawns and shrimps.

Frank Sawyer's Nymphing Secrets

LIGHT TACKLE

With me I had my 10ft. 6 in. grease-line outfit, a rod built on the principle of my Trout Nymphing rod and which I use mostly for sea trout. A number 4 D.T. trout line and a cast tapered to 8lb breaking strain made it complete. Light tackle is necessary for the method I had in mind to try. With me I had some of my grayling lure patterns made up on No. 3 low-water, salmon hooks, and so, with one of these knotted on securely, I went into action.

Maybe, in view of what followed I will be condemned for using such light tackle. My excuse is that this was in the form of an experiment for I wished to prove what I had long suspected – that stale fish such as these are not impossible to catch.

From the bridge parapet it was quite easy to cast, for the pool is on the downstream side. My method of attack was to drop the bug well upstream of a fish, let it sink down and drift to a point just in front and slightly below the level of a salmon, and then lift the rod point so that the lure was pulled upwards to swing past the nose of the fish.

I concentrated my efforts on one of about 15 lb which was clearly visible and lying high in the water. This fish was interested at once and just for a moment I thought he might take the first cast I made near enough for him to see. Time and again he moved forward, then suddenly, after I had tried him quite twenty times he moved forward and took with a quick snap. The hook held but he was a lively fish and after three or four minutes of excitement he went around a well-known snag in the middle of the pool and the cast parted. This was the start of a day of success and failure.

FIVE FISH TOOK

Five of the seven fish took the grayling lure in much the same way and these included the monster of the pool. He, like the 15-pounder, took very suddenly after I had been tempting him and another one much smaller which was lying close to him. Just a quick move forwards and a snap of the jaws.

I think I deserved to kill this big fish. For just over half an hour I had complete control and had there been a place where I could have got him in near enough to reach with the gaff, all would have been well. As it was, a large group of onlookers, including my two friends, had a perfect view of the tiring out of a big salmon with a light rod.

CAST BROKE

He was beaten and on his side when I tried to tow him over a wide fringe of weeds to the only landing place. The strain was just too much. My light rod bent almost double and owing to a barbed wire fence a yard or so behind me, I could move him no nearer. Down went his head and he bored downwards into the weed, my cast broke near the eye of the hook. The keeper has not exaggerated. I think the first might well have weighed 40 lb and to have landed such a one on an 8 lb breaking strain cast point would indeed have been a triumph.

Disappointing as it was, that day has given me plenty to think about. As I have said I hooked five of the seven salmon which I could see in the pool. Three were only lightly hooked, and after only a moment or two which gave me the thrill of feeding their first pull, came unstuck. Maybe I needed a slightly larger hook, or perhaps did not strike hard enough to get the barb well in. The thing which matters most, is that each took the lure and I feel sure that here is a technique which might well be developed and which may lead to a chance for good sport with fish which so far have been considered hopeless.

With grayling and trout I have found through the years that only one colour is successful. It is very important that the correct shape is used. Strangely enough the wool is one which is not used frequently and therefore the colour is difficult to obtain. "Chadwicks" list it as colour 477 but only when wet has it the shade which attracts the fish.

Making the lure is a job any tyro can do. First a hook of the desired size. Over the shank, from eye to bend, wind a double layer of silver-coloured 5 amp. Fuse wire, and aim to build up the hook into an elongated hump back. Then over this put a double covering of the wool. Secure the wool with a couple of turns of the wire and a double hitch either at hook end, or behind the eye, and cut off spare ends neatly. A minute perhaps, and the job is complete, and yet there is something which may give you a chance to land a 40-pounder.

Fishing through the years with nymphs for trout and grayling has taught me just what a fish expects to see, and though the correct colour and construction of nymphs and lures is necessary, far more important is the manner of presentation. Here lies the secret of success.

INSTINCT TO SNAP

To me it appeared that the salmon, like many trout and grayling, were interested only when something drifting in the water suddenly checks and appears to swim towards the surface. The instinct to snap and catch seems to be irresistible and the angler has only to tighten at the right moment.

As I have said, my view from the bridge parapet was good. It was possible to see the fish and to judge the exact moment to check the lure and make it swim. It was also easy to see the fish move forward and the opening and closing of the jaws. It was very much like nymph fishing for visible trout. Perhaps this made it simple, but I do think that in pools where a number of salmon are congregated, that one or another could be caught by fishing the lure blindly. By this I mean to cast out, allow the bug to sink well down, then give a lift with the rod point and watch for the draw of the cast.

SINK QUICKLY

A well-greased line and a long cast tapered to a fine point are essential. It is necessary for the lure to sink quickly. It can do this only on a light-weight cast. An outfit balanced to meet all requirements is also a must. Most important is a rod with a sensitive tip with which one can strike sharply and firmly without danger of breaking when the hook takes hold. The rod too must be single-handed and light.

Though the technique is very similar to nymph fishing for trout and grayling, I think it should be described in a different way. Whatever the fish mistake the lure for, most certainly it is not a nymph of the *Ephemeroptera*. Maybe they take it for the larvae of the big sedges *P. grandis* or *P. striata*, or think it is just an outsize of some of the smaller types.

Periodically we get what I call a boost in grayling production when far greater numbers of fry survive than in average years. One of these came in 1973 and all through that year, from June onwards, the river teemed with hordes of these little fish, all much too small to net in the autumn and then, last year, when we had planned to thin them out, we had continuous high and dirty water. Netting had to be abandoned. In consequence we had to begin this season with grayling spread all about the river, and they rose madly to every hatch of fly.

When I wrote my spring report, I warned our members that this could happen, and made the request that they should all try to catch as many grayling as they could. This request was well carried out, and I find on checking the monthly returns that well over 3,000 were taken by rods from the six-mile stretch of the fishery. A fair number were killed in early season on the dry-fly but the great majority were taken with nymphs in the later months. My son Tim did his share on the few occasions he was home and during one weekend he took a total of 150. As I have said, these were mostly small, third-summer fish, which have a length of about 10 inches. He used my Killer Bug, a pattern I devised many years ago purposely for taking grayling. It is as deadly now as it was then, and must have accounted for many thousands of grayling, and indeed other fish, in the meantime.

Tim really enjoys fishing the Bug for grayling and he has the quick reflex action which is so necessary to be able to hook them. If you go the right way about fishing for them, take they will. I don't fish a great deal myself when Tim is home, as I get a lot of satisfaction by watching him. I am quite happy to act as ghilie: to take the fish as he swings them to land and to knock them on the head and remove the hook. We seldom use a landing net for with most of these little grayling it is possible to lift them clear of the water with the rod, without fear of damage. A few will come off and escape, but generally, if you wait for fish to stop wriggling and lift out smoothly, you land most.

As I have said, I like to watch Tim in action. First his care in approach to avoid any scare of the shoal, or individual, as the case might be; the trial delivery of the Bug to see what reaction there is to the fall of leader and line. Then, if he is satisfied, comes the first real cast which has his full attention.

He has learned to pitch the Bug into the water with the least disturbance possible and then comes the quick gathering of all slack line and at the same time getting the rod into a comfortable position. His eyes, like mine, watch the point just where the floating leader goes beneath the water. There comes a check in the drift of the leader and a little twitch as a fish takes and, quick as a flash, back and up goes the rod tip. Invariably I say "yes" when I see the take, but by the time I have uttered the word, the rod is bending.

Tim is successful simply because he is quick with the rod. But you can only be fast if you have tackle that you can use speedily, and this means a light quick-actioned rod with a light line and leader. There is never any need to cast long distances for if you are careful in approach and select the right angle, a cast of about 15 paces is plenty to take at a distance far beyond this, but for each one you hook at least a dozen are missed completely, or just pricked.

A few years ago I had the great pleasure of helping a very dear old friend of mine to catch a few fish when he had given up hope of ever being able to hook another grayling. His eyesight had been failing gradually for a long time and he had got to the stage when he could no longer see anything distinctly. In the past we had spend many hours together both fishing and shooting. He had invited me to a day after pheasants about the middle of October and I had stayed on to have tea with him and wife and to chatter of old times.

As might be expected, we started talking about grayling-catching with the Bug after the trout season was over. I could tell by the tone of his voice and the wistfulness in his expression that his thoughts were on some of the pools we had fished together in the past, and suddenly the thought occurred to me that I could be his eyes. I felt sure, if he could be quick enough to tighten, that we had a chance.

And so I made the suggestion that he should get his man to bring him to my house the following day where I would have my rod ready and we could spend a couple of hours on a pool where I knew there were a fair number of decent-sized grayling. He was delighted, and so was his wife. As she said afterwards, "I prayed that he might catch one a least."

It was a lovely clear, sunny day and my friend was punctual to the minute. Arrangements were quickly made for his driver to pick him up at a certain time and I packed the tackle he had brought, together with his shooting stick, into my car and then got my own gear, which I thought might be lighter and quicker than his. I could tell he was excited and anxious to be at the riverside to have a try.

The pool I had selected to try was some 60 feet long and about the same in width. In its deepest part it was about five feet. I chose a place on the bank from which I could see clearly to the bottom and the movement of all the fish. Also I had cleared all herbage which might interfere with a back-cast.

I need not have worried much about the casting, for my friend knew how to hold a line high behind. I placed his shooting stick firmly where he could sit and face the direction I wanted him to cast to, and then gave him my rod and instructions. As I spoke to him I could see that the fish were in no way alarmed by our presence on the bank. I saw several moving here and there to take nymphs, and an occasional one came to the surface for a fly. I knew then that we did indeed have a chance.

I put on a Killer Bug which I had constructed to sink quickly, then I briefed him as to procedure. He had to make two false casts so that I could alter his direction if necessary, and then make his delivery. He was to gather in all slack line after a slight pause, then lift his rod tip when I said lift. If I said "yes", he must strike immediately. My instructions were followed perfectly. The Bug pitched in and sank quickly just upstream of two of the largest fish in the pool. As it went down, I could see my friend had gathered in the slack. As I glanced back at the fish one came up from the bottom to take, and I shouted "yes!" just as he opened his mouth.

His response was instant. The quick though gentle flick of the rod tip set the hook as the jaws closed, and our first fish, a grayling of 1½ lb, was on. In a few moments he had guided it to the bank where I netted it. Though it is true that a number of small fish took and rejected far too quickly for him to act, we caught six more, all over a pound, which held just that fraction longer. I found that if I said "yes" just before the fish actually took, the timing to hook was perfect. But I must admit that there were a number which turned away just as I expected a take, and so there was no connection when he tightened to my command.

The following week he came again and this time caught five. His wife phoned to say how delighted she was and that he had talked of little else. As she said, it was something for him to think about and to prove that his fishing days were not over. Alas, and sad to say, he never came again, for two days afterwards he had a stroke, and died the same evening. But I like to think that he got some satisfaction and pleasure in catching those fish, just as I did by making it possible.

Footnotes

1 The fresh grayling is reported to have a thyme-like flavour or smell, hence the Latin name *Thymallus Thymallus.* In the summer my family sometimes get together for a barbecue down by Tank Crossing Bravo on the Avon. During the morning we catch several small grayling then gut them at the riverside. When barbequed in the open air with a white wine, olive oil and herb marinade, they are quite superb.

2 Chadwick's 477 is so rare and valuable that it may not be wise to 'waste' it on Killer Bugs. The wool is a collector's item and fishermen have been known to leave original 477 in their wills. There is no doubt that the original 477 wool had magical properties; unfortunately production ceased decades ago.

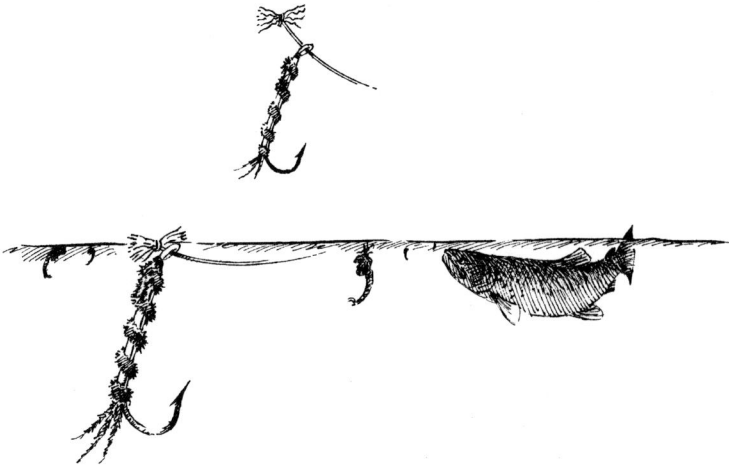

FISHING THE BOW TIE BUZZER

Taken from a series of articles in *Shooting Times and Country Magazine* – 1975

Though I wrote a few articles earlier about general nymph fishing I made no mention in them of fishing the buzzer; this is something I ought to remedy, because I think that fishing a good representation of this particular insect can be really fascinating and, in a way, even more skilful than the ordinary nymphing technique. I have never been able to find out who christened this creature but understand that it was linked mostly with Blagdon Lake in Somerset and named as the Blagdon Buzzer. Which of the three or four species – black, red or green – this referred to, is impossible to say. All one can state with truth is that they all belong to the *chironomid* family and have habits that are almost identical.

The name "buzzer" could have originated from the noise these creatures make with their wings when they gather together in big assemblies during their premating dance. On occasions, many thousands will dance and weave in great spirals high above the ground and form what one might be forgiven for thinking was a queer-shaped cloud. All the while there is the humming or buzzing noise. These are the males and if you watch closely you can see individual females entering the swarm and mating taking place. Then they, the females, leave to go egg-laying on the water. The eggs are laid by dipping in much the same way as some of the *ephemeroptera* species. Though this could be one explanation, there is another, for often when hatching in open water, the insect will buzz around on the surface and often skitter along it before taking flight.

For some reason I have never been able to understand, fish are not greatly interested in the actual fly, whether in freshly hatched form, or in the perfect stage, when the females are about the water for egg-laying. But it is an entirely different question when the larvae, or nymph, as one might as well call it. Today the buzzer is well known to all who fish lakes and reservoirs. And what is well known also is the frustration one can experience at late evening when a big hatch occurs. I know it is a lovely sight when a flat calm surface of a lake suddenly becomes distorted with the rise forms of fish, and just how excited one can become when seeing heads, dorsals and tail fins, breaking the water, as trout after trout comes within casting distance. Yes, it can bring the feeling that at any moment a big fellow will make a mistake. But for a very long time this did not happen for me, and perhaps it would not happen now but for an idea which came to my mind while fashioning yet another artificial to try.

Previous to this I had made up a number of different patterns and tried them without much success. Indeed I had always left knowing the fish had beaten me; that the ones I had caught were more by luck than due to my skill as a fly dresser.

I came to know these nymphs very well and though I had made up a number of artificials which I thought were very reasonable copies of the naturals, something the trout expected to see was missing. I had a good idea in my mind what this was, for I had watched many of these nymphs while they were in the process of eclosion. In one of his books Skues was pleased to quote Halford as saying of a certain river nymph that, though it might be possible to copy the actual nymph, it was "impossible" to imitate its wriggle".

Now this is quite true of several of the *ephemeropteran* nymphs, one in particular being that of the blue-winged olive. Maybe this was the one Halford had in mind. Much the same thing could have been said of the buzzer nymph.

Buzzer nymphs do not swim in the same sense as those of the up-winged class of insects. Their movement from the bottom to the surface is mostly in a vertical plane and their travel through the water is accomplished by a series of contractions of the body when the fringed parts of head and tail come together in a kind of loop. In fact they loop themselves through the water in much the same way as the gnat larvae one can see in most static waters, in water butts, puddles and ponds. These, of course, are of the same family – only much smaller. These creatures have no legs which show loosely. The legs are contained inside the integument which is sloughed at the time of emergence to a fly; so legs are not a feature one needs to include in a dressing.

But something that is very noticeable is the white celia, or fringe or minute hairs, at the head part of the nymph. These are appendages which have no function after the nymph has hatched and are still attached to the shuck when this is cast. I make particular mention of this because there are times when hundreds of these shucks, with their white fringes, can be seen floating, and anyone inexperienced could be forgiven for thinking these are actual nymphs. But, even if we can be deceived, the trout are not. What they look for is something which shows movement, a wriggling movement, something among the shucks which looks alive.

An exact copy of the nymph, including the white celia, was not good enough, for the difficulty lay in fishing this so that it appeared natural. The very action of these creatures in ascending almost vertically ruled out any lifelike horizontal movement being transmitted by a rod, for such a movement as this would cause immediate suspicion. What was needed was an artificial made so that it could be cast delicately, so that it could penetrate the surface and then hang, more or less, in suspension beneath it. At the same time this must show some sign of life which could attract a cruising fish. Not an easy problem to solve as no doubt you will agree. Yet, when I did hit upon the idea it was really simple. In a future article I will tell you all about it and the way it is fished.

Fishing the buzzer nymph is a technique different from all other known methods of fly or nymph fishing and success or failure with it depends to a very great extent on two factors. First of these lies in the construction of an artificial pattern which, without any movement imparted to it by the angler, can delude fish into thinking it is a living creature. Secondly, and of even more importance, is in the manner of its presentation so that it can appear in the water just where the trout expect to see it.

Actually one could call it a cross between dry-fly and float fishing. Dry-fly in the manner of casting, and float fishing as regards watching for a take. Maybe there are some who will say it is a boring occupation compared with the cast and search methods; carried out with wet-fly and general lure fishing. But I have found it to be fascinating and, at times, very rewarding for the patience one must have.

As I have said many times, simplicity in fishing is the aim to be pursued. This is doubly true when it comes to dressing flies and nymphs. The main thing is to be able to assess from the trout's point of view and then create accordingly. It was very easy to see by the leisurely way in which trout approached and took this kind of prey that no escape of the insect was anticipated, and it became increasingly obvious that fish expected a characteristic which differed from the great majority of the creatures they are in the habit of taking in and just beneath the surface of the water.

The Sawyer pattern now known as the Bow Tie Buzzer was the result of my general observations, and a full explanation of the tying and the materials used in the creation of this article can be seen on page 63 of my book *Nymphs and the Trout*. I have no intention of repeating this here but I think I can claim that the idea of using the white fringe on the leader as a separate part is original. However, there has been a little confusion about the proper rigging of this nymph and perhaps a few words about this, and the correct manner of fishing it, will be of help. My tying is designed to represent the reddish-yellow type of buzzer which I think are the most common but, whether one dresses up bodies to simulate the black or the green ones, the separate bow tie at the end of the leader can be used. All these nymphs are large and can be fashioned on hooks of size 3 in the old scale, or No. 12 in new scale.

We always use down-eyed hooks because then the little bow tie can seat into the eye at the top. What is more, this allows the nymph to hang properly in the water. Our buzzer nymphs are on cards and sold in packets of six. One of the six is rigged with an example of the bow tie on a short piece of nylon drawn into the top part of the hook eye. As I have said, this is purely for example, but I make mention of it because some people have joined this short piece of nylon to the end of their leader instead of using a part of the wool provided to make their own bow tie.

The important thing is to thread up through the hook eye, then disregard the actual nymph on the leader and fashion a slip-knot at the end of the tippet. Put a piece of wool into the slip-knot and pull the knot tight. Then with a sharp pair of scissors, cut away all but a tiny bit which should be held firmly in the knot. A small piece is enough, just sufficient to prevent it from pulling through the eye of the hook. If you make the bow too big the general effect is ruined and fish refuse to take. When rigged properly the bow tie should seat nicely in the hook eye when the nymph is slid down to it, and yet it should be free to move. The actual hook eye of the nymph is free on the leader and so rigged that it can wobble from side to side or spin completely round as though swivelled. This combination of movement is sufficient to delude fish into thinking the nymph is alive. The correct rigging is the secret for success because, like a dry-fly, no movement can be imparted to it after being cast.

Casting and general presentation is very much like dry-fly work and for it one needs a good quality floating line. Even so, it is wise to well grease two thirds of the leader so that this too can float high on the water where the buoyancy can help to stop the nymph from sinking more than a foot or so. The floating part of the leader also acts as the indicator of a take and after a cast has been made full attention should be directed to it.

Cast lightly and delicately, bearing in mind that all you need to do is make the nymph penetrate the surface in the area where fish are feeding. From then on no movement of the rod and line should be made. In this kind of fishing you do nothing to try to attract the eyes of your quarry. This part is taken care of with the construction of the nymph and its bow tie.

When feeding on buzzer nymphs, still water trout cruise about a large area. Nothing is accomplished by continuous

CONSTRUCTION OF BOW TIE BUZZER.

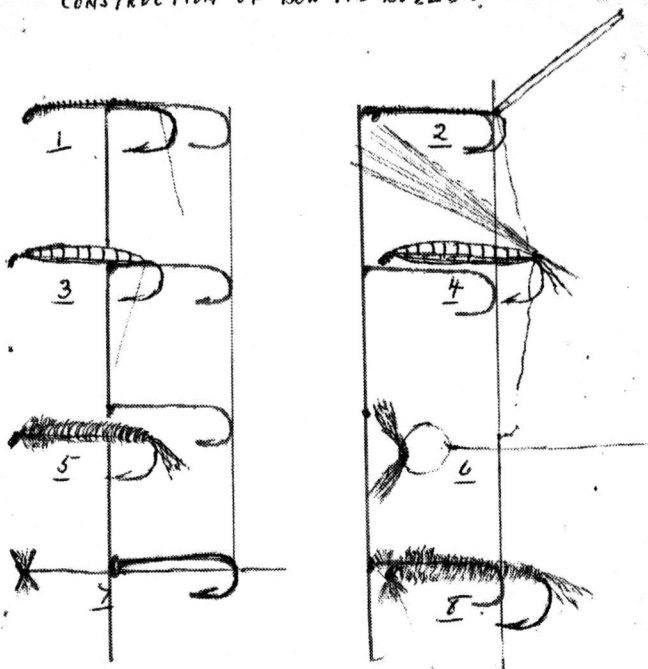

FIGS.

1. AN EVEN WINDING OF WIRE
2. TYING IN STRIP OF FOIL.
3. FOIL WOUND ON HOOK FOR BASE
4. TYING IN PHEASANT TAIL FIBRES FOR TAIL AND BODY.
5. FIBRES LAPPED OVER FOIL
6. SLIP KNOT IN LEADER TO ATTACH BOW TIE
7. BOW TIE KNOTTED AND SHAPED WITH HOOK THREADED
8. BOW TIE IN POSITION. WITH NYLON LEADER THROUGH EYE.

*Frank Sawyer's original drawing on how to construct
the Bow Tie Buzzer.*

recasting. Just allow the nymph to hang and then be patient. Wait for the fish to come and always hold your rod in a comfortable position to be able to strike quickly and firmly. Recast only when it is thought that the nymph has sunk too deep.

Fish can see the hanging nymph through the water for a distance of quite ten feet, but mostly they look for these nymphs in the upper part of the water and once an artificial has sunk below the level at which the fish are feeding it ceases to be attractive. Usually a take by a fish is well defined by the sudden draw of the floating leader, and it is this one must watch for intently. However, even though there are times when the downward draw can be caused by a sudden sinking of the nymph, my advice, unless you can see there is no fish in the locality, is to tighten and think afterwards. Sometimes a take can be barely perceptible.

Most stillwater fishermen, I feel sure, will agree with me when I say that of all the aquatic creatures which excite trout into rising, the buzzers have been the most frustrating to represent, both in the construction of an artificial and in the successful fishing of it. Many and varied are the patterns I have seen and tried and many are those I have evolved myself which I thought would give me confidence when fishing, but to no avail. This went on until about four years ago when I put into practice an idea that had been in my mind for a long time. It is with pleasure and with a certain satisfaction that I pass the idea on to those why may be interested in giving it a trial.

We have named this pattern "The Bow Tie Buzzer". This was a name suggested for it by an old friend who had tried it with success in the West Country and it is a name which I think will be remembered. I had made enough different patterns of buzzers to know that it was not just a good copy of the natural that was required. I knew too, that when these creatures were hatching, it was almost useless to try to interest fish in a representation of anything else. The fish got their eye in, in a manner of speaking, and looked for that one something they expected to see. Shape and general colouration was not enough.

The trouble was that the deception could not be helped by a movement of rod and line, as is the case with the majority of nymphs and other representations of creatures which swim, or make a horizontal movement through the water. Buzzer nymphs cannot swim in this sense; their movement to or from the surface is mostly in a vertical plane, upwards and downwards, not through the water. They have no real legs or setae to act as propulsion units. The manner of ascent or descent is by a series of loops or convulsions, a wriggle more than any straightforward swimming.

Because of this and because also these nymphs have a habit of hanging in mid-water and at the surface, I found it to be extremely difficult to incorporate anything in the tying which could simulate movement, the kind of movement a fish expects to see.

Then it occurred to me to try a nymph in two parts. One of the main features of the buzzer is the white fringe, or celia, present at the front of the head. This shows very prominently when the nymphs are about to hatch and is in continuous movement. And I felt, if I made this separately, and so that it could have free movement in the water, that I would accomplish something worthwhile. Then it struck me that this could be carried on the end of the leader. A little bow tie in fact, which could move in the eye of the hook. At the same time I accomplished something else for, with this attachment, the nymph could hang almost vertically in the water and, if so desired, the body could be made to spin around the leader.

So now the secret, if indeed it is a secret, is out. All you have to do is to make up a nymph body of a size, shape and colouration to suit the natural, and then make up the bow at the end of the leader at the time you want to fish.

However, making up the body is no simple matter if it is to look similar to a natural about to hatch which, of course, is the time when the fish go mad to take. At this time the whole appearance of the creature changes from a dull, almost drab effect to one that is translucent, almost luminous. The whole body has a sheen of silver along it which makes it show up very plainly in the water. This seems to shine through the integument almost like a light and brings out the main colours. The silvery appearance is accentuated as the shuck of the insect is being thrust clear of the body and in my tying I have tried to incorporate this effect. The partially slipped shuck is represented by body fibres draping the hook bend.

The accompanying drawings show the sequence of construction and the manner of making the bow tie in the leader. All that is needed is a description of the materials. The wire used is gold coloured over which is lapped a strip of silver foil. This acts for the base. Then tie in four fibres of browny red cock pheasant tail. Tie in the fine ends so these can act as the slipping shuck, then dress over the silver foil so that the sheen from it can show through. Build up the head end to a hump and finish off the tying behind the eye.

The bow tie can be fashioned from a piece of white nylon wool. The hook size most suitable is No. 3, old scale or 12 on the new scale. The down eye is preferable. Thread end of leader upwards through hook eye of nymph, then disregard it. Fashion a slip knot at the end of leader and pull this tightly on to the piece of wool. Trim with sharp scissors to make the little bow. Care should be taken not to make the bow too big. Afterwards the nymph can be slid up to the bow and all is ready to start fishing. If tied correctly the bow cannot be pulled through the hook eye. The weight of the nymph holds it in position while casting and a slight tightening of the line after a cast has been made will ensure the bow is in the right position. Hanging as it does on the leader makes no difference in the hooking of fish; indeed such a position usually gives a very secure hold.

I have used the tying in many different waters and have had great success and sport with it. I have found no difficulty in making the bow tie, indeed the tying of a slip knot and trimming of the bow takes no longer than attaching a leader in the ordinary way. I hope my experiences will be yours also.

HOW TO TIE A PHEASANT TAIL NYMPH

The following series of photos are taken from the only surviving piece of film showing Frank Sawyer actually tying one of his famous Pheasant Tail Nymphs. The technique is exactly the same for the Grey Goose and Sawyer Swedish.

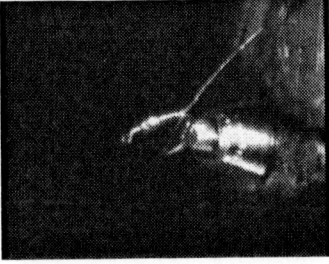
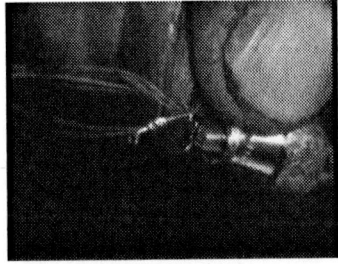

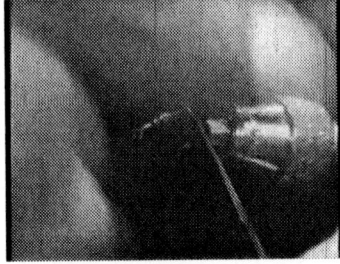
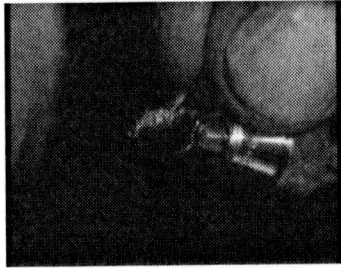
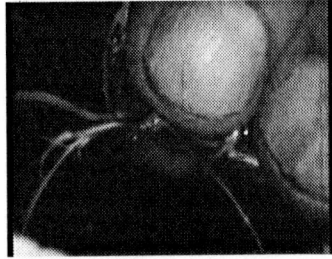
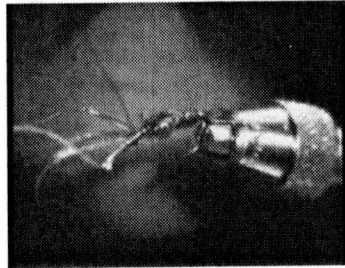
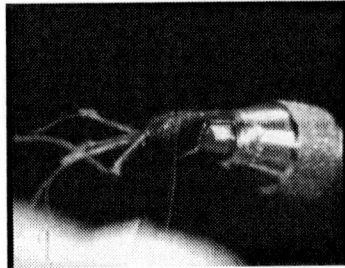

How to Tie a Pheasant Tail Nymph

79

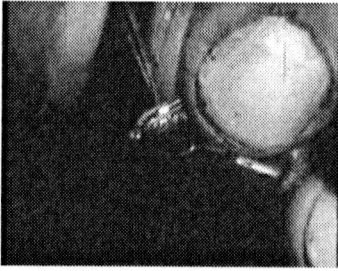

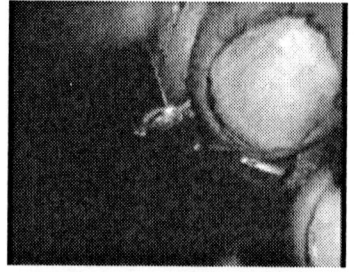

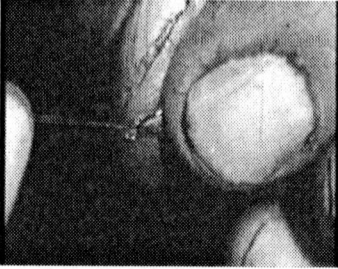

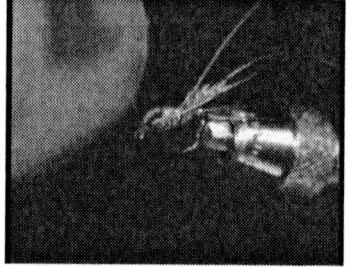

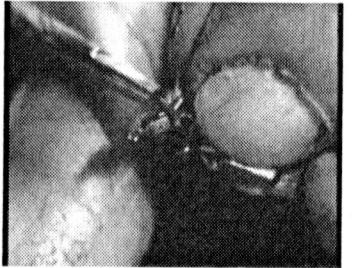

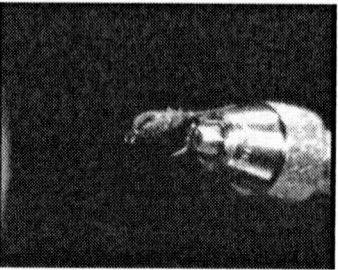

How to Tie a Pheasant Tail Nymph

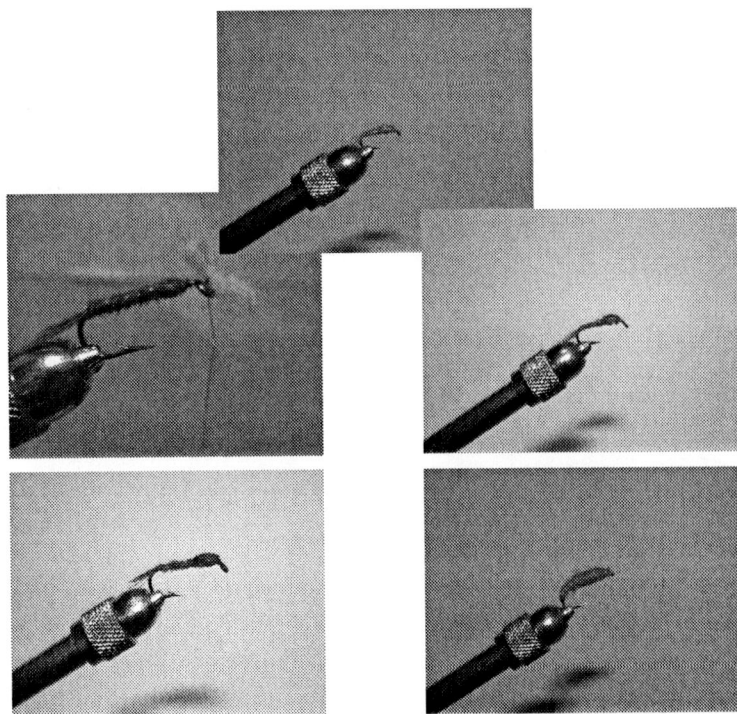

FRANK SAWYER NYMPHS

Nick Sawyer is proud to offer nymphs tied in the original manner devised by his grandfather the late Frank Sawyer MBE.

All nymphs £6 per dozen including UK p&p. For overseas orders and credit cards please use the website www.sawyernymphs.com

Please order by writing the number of dozens required in the relevant size/type box and mail with a cheque payable to Sawyer Nymphs Ltd, 45 Moberly Road, Salisbury SP1 3BZ. Unfortunately we cannot split dozens at present.

	10	12	14	16	18	20
PTN						
GG						
SS						
SKB				N/A	N/A	N/A
BTB			N/A	N/A	N/A	N/A
Mixed	N/A		N/A	N/A	N/A	N/A

Nymphs and the Trout
by Frank Sawyer (2006 edition)

A special limited edition of 1000 individually numbered books. Volume consists of 1958 first edition and 1970 second revised edition plus a new additional chapter.
Quality buckram hardback with marble slipcase.

£50 including UK p&p

Keeper of the Stream
by Frank Sawyer (2006 edition)

A special limited edition of 1000 individually numbered books. New introduction by Frank's only son Tim, a brand new chapter of previously unpublished material and 8 pages of photographs.
Quality buckram hardback with marble slipcase.

£40 including UK p&p.

Also available:

Fishing on the Front Line by Nick Sawyer. Personal accounts of fishing and soldiering with the modern British Army. Hardback, £15.95 including UK p&p

Buy *Keeper of the Stream* and *Nymphs and the Trout* and get *Fishing on the Front Line* free!

Sawyer Nymphs Ltd, 45 Moberly Road, Salisbury, SP1 3BZ. Overseas and credit card orders through the website at www.sawyernymphs.com Please note that offers are only available through mail order with the form overleaf.

Sawyer Nymphs Ltd, 45 Moberly Road, Salisbury, SP1 3BZ

☐   Nymphs and the Trout (£50 inc P&P)
☐   Keeper of the Stream (£40 inc P&P)
☐   Fishing on the Front Line (£15.95 inc P&P)

Sum enclosed............ (cheques made payable to Sawyer Nymphs Ltd)

Please charge my credit card: Card................................ Signature.................

Card no................................Expiry date............ Signature.................

Issue Number .... (for Switch cards only)

Deliver to: Card Name & address if different:

NAME.................................... NAME....................................

ADDRESS............................... ADDRESS...............................

....

....

Postcode............Tel................ Postcode............Tel................

Sawyer Nymphs

Printed in the United Kingdom
by Lightning Source UK Ltd.
116004UKS00001B/68